THE TEN MINUTE TEAM

10 Steps to Building High Performing Teams

Thomas Isgar, Ph. D.

Seluera Press

Boulder, Colorado

Library of Congress Catalog Card Number: 89-62354

ISBN 0-9623464-1-1

First Printing September, 1989
Second Printing March, 1990
Third Printing February, 1991
Fourth Printing January, 1992

Second Edition
First Printing July, 1993

Printed in U.S.A.

Photo—back cover by Sherman Grinnell

CONTENTS

ACKNOWLEDGMENTS

The value of teams was never more clear than when as an author I attempted a cover design. After weeks of doodling I asked a team of colleagues to work on a design based on my specifications. They quickly developed several new ideas and then, with me having one vote, selected the cover of this book.

No book gets to market without significant effort and support on the part of many people. This book is the product of hundreds of team members and team leaders. Their efforts and struggles to move toward high performance provide the real life lessons captured within.

Without the Womanpower of Kathy Terrill and Bobbie Eggleston this book would still be in a file. With energy, optimism and competence, Marie Mandrack took this work from manuscript to finished book.

Susan and Aaron's support and encouragement throughout was invaluable.

Dick Batten, Manufacturing Human Capital Strategy Manager at Polaroid Corporation was very helpful by suggesting numerous detailed changes in this printing.

INTRODUCTION TO THE
SECOND EDITION

Time flies...

The first edition of *The Ten Minute Team* was published four years ago. Aware of the stigma of *apparent* obsolescence, we consulted with our customers (which include Fortune 500 companies, universities and government agencies) and found that they were happy with the book as it was and sales have steadily increased.

We conclude that making some minor editorial changes, thereby changing the publication date, is our best move. We know that the book is as valid today as when it was written, yet we also know that some would by-pass *The Ten Minute Team* on the basis of the original publication date alone.

So, if you have purchased a second edition of *The Ten Minute Team* hoping for new information, and are disappointed, write to us. You can reach us at Seluera, Inc., PO Box 868, Boulder, Colorado 80306-0868.

Thomas Isgar
Sarasota, Florida
1993

INTRODUCTION

This book is about a new team leader's search for the skills to develop a High Performing Team. It is also about a superior manager who has developed techniques for turning her employees into a high performing team. She knows the value of working with individuals but has found that the work often calls for her and her employees to work as a team. She is like most other managers in this respect.

Teams, task forces or work groups are part of organizations at all levels. Many organizations spend large sums of money working to improve the effectiveness of individual teams. Some provide team development workshops. Others offer sessions to build teams, usually called *team building*.

Organizations often rely on models from professional sports to attempt to understand the dynamics of their work teams. While this is helpful, not all workers identify with sports teams. Some don't even like sports.

Thus, over several years and numerous experiments this manager has evolved a set of beliefs about the requirements for developing a high performing team. She has also developed some simple, ten minute activities to develop her own high performing team. It is from these activities that the name Ten Minute Team arose.

Her teams have been able to exceed their goals over long time periods. Her team is consistently recognized by others in the organization as being a winning team. Equally important, her team members have received individual recognition. Finally, team members report that being a member of this manager's team is both an exciting and growing experience.

While this book uses a manufacturing setting, the beliefs and activities provide a practical set of steps any manager or team leader can use in any setting to develop her or his own high performing team.

If your team is non-traditional the team leader would help the team focus on the elements of high performance. If your team has no designated leader then team members could ask the team to focus on the elements of high performance.

The first chapter introduces the reader to the cast of characters and to an overview of the model for understanding high performing teams. The model provides a structure for the remaining chapters. Each chapter contains a summary of the key points in boldface. In addition, each chapter contains specific activities a team leader can use to improve her/his team's performance. All the key points are summarized at the end of the book. The material in this book is a summary of years of experience with teams—as a member, leader and developer.

Often, important learnings are discovered only after the learner goes on a search for knowledge, encounters obstacles, has marvelous insights and finally arrives back at the beginning transformed from the journey. This book takes you on a search to discover the steps for developing high performing teams. While the learner is a new supervisor and the guide is an experienced and rare manager who knows the steps to developing high performing teams, the seeker is really all of us who are struggling to increase the level of performance in our teams.

Thomas Isgar
Boulder, Colorado
1989

THE SUPERVISOR, THE MANAGER, AND THE TEN MINUTE TEAM

After receiving his promotion, the new supervisor was immediately confronted with leading a team. Because he was ambitious he wanted to discover the steps required to develop a high performing team. Wherever he looked, inside organizations and out, there were teams, task forces, committees, boards, work groups, departments, sections, and branches. Each of them seemed to be struggling to carry out its tasks as a team.

He decided the approach to follow would be to read all he could about teams. His enthusiasm waned, however, as soon as he began to review the numerous articles, books and research studies on teams. As many as fifty different factors were held out as the secret to developing high performing teams. They ranged from placing the entire team in a therapy group to relying on inspirational "locker room talks" from the team leader. Several studies reported similar factors but even these were labeled differently. "Open communication" sounded like "on-going dialog," which sounded like "high-level verbal interaction," which sounded like "information exchanges." However, the supervisor couldn't be sure. What seemed missing in all the studies was a clear model of a high performing team with a description of the actual steps the team leader could use to obtain high performance.

With some reluctance the supervisor decided to talk to a few real managers. He wasn't very optimistic because in his experience most teams weren't high performing, and most managers didn't place a very high priority on developing their teams. In addition, talking to managers was going to take days. He began by asking his old boss, other supervisors and friends in other companies to recommend managers whose teams were exceptional. He wasn't surprised when several people said that they didn't know anyone who could help. Some recommended that he study professional sports teams. However, to his surprise one manager at another location in his own organization was recommended by several people. They told him to ask about the Ten Minute Team.

He decided to call her to arrange a meeting. He was very pleased when she returned his first call and expressed interest in his question about teamwork. An appointment was made for the next week.

As the Supervisor drove to the appointment he wondered about this Manager who was reputed to have developed a high performing team. Would she be tough, in the Vince Lombardi tradition, like some male managers he knew? Would she be inspirational like John Kennedy? Would she be articulate and outspoken like Geraldine Ferraro? Finally, he wondered if high performing teams were the result of a particular style of leadership. He also wondered briefly if women might be better at developing high performing teams.

After being cleared by the receptionist, he was directed to the office of the Manager where the secretary was expecting him. The secretary buzzed the Manager and was asked to admit the Supervisor. The Manager rose with a smile and extended her hand. She had a firm handshake and confident manner. At first glance, however, the Supervisor didn't see anything which might explain why this particular Manager could develop high performing teams.

"I called for this appointment because you were described as having a high performing work group. I want to know if you can tell me how you develop a high performing team," the Supervisor said.

"Before we begin that discussion, tell me something about yourself," said the Manager.

"Well, ah, I'm a very new supervisor," he stammered.

"I know that, and that your name is Larry," the Manager responded. "Tell me some more about your background."

"Well, I went to State College and studied materials management and process engineering. I went to work for a large oil company as an engineer and stayed for three years. I've been at the West plant for four years in a manufacturing group. I play softball for the company and in the city league. I'm married with one daughter who is five years old. But, I seem to be working all the time."

"I understand that," replied the Manager with a chuckle. "As you know my name is Patricia, but most of my colleagues call me Pat. They think that makes me one of the boys.

"We have several things in common. I also went to State College, but a few years before you. I was one of the first women Electrical Engineering graduates. I got married my senior year and have two children, both in college.

"I've been with this company for nearly 16 years. I started as an analyst in the engineering group, became a project engineer, then was the supervisor of an engineering group for three years. The company sponsored me in a ten week Executive Program at the University. After that I became manager of Corporate Engineering for four years. Three years ago I was asked to manage our production department, which includes an accounting group and an engineering group as well as manufacturing."

After a pause the Manager said, reflectively, "Each job has been bigger and each has convinced me even more that effective management requires building an effective team.

"When I began as a supervisor I didn't receive any training in supervision. But, I knew that if I was to suc- ceed, I had to have my employees pull together and pull in the same direction. That's where my interest in teams began. Since then I have read a lot about team development, attended training programs and talked to my colleagues. More importantly, however, I have tried lots of new techniques to see if I can improve the long term performance of my team."

"That is what I want to learn about!" exclaimed the Supervisor.

"Before we begin that discussion," the Manager said, "I hope you understand the importance of time manage- ment, goal setting, and coaching each of your employ- ees. In fact, those skills provided me with the free time I needed to think about how to improve the performance of my team."

"I know all about time management," said Larry. "My manager is a good time manager and by learning from him I have found time to meet with you. I'm good at goal setting and I'm getting better at coaching. However, I don't think the teams I'm part of perform at their best. There must be something else."

"An important addition is understanding that being a good supervisor of individuals will not build a team. You must begin to focus on the team and work less one to one," replied the Manager.

"There are other steps to developing a high performing team," she continued. "However, the basic skills provide a good start. Once you have mastered them, you should have the relationship base and the performance base to ask the team to engage in a set of developmental steps to increase its performance."

"That's what I came to find out about!" the Supervisor exclaimed again. "This is going to be easier than I imagined," he thought as he opened his note pad. "What is the first step?" he asked.

"Before we begin the discussion, I would like to have you meet my team," Patricia replied. "Do you have the time?"

*　　*　　*　　*　　*

The team held its meetings in a small conference room because the Manager believed that a setting more neutral than her office helped the team members be more open. The first thing Larry noticed was that all of the team members were engaged in an animated discussion about the budget. The second thing he noticed was that all of the members were on time. The Manager introduced Larry and told the team why he was with them. She also asked that they be available to answer any questions he might have.

The team appeared like many other work teams Larry had encountered. He wasn't sure what he had expected. This team seemed more lively and maybe they were a little more friendly. Otherwise they were the usual mix of age, sex and race. As the Manager asked them to introduce themselves, he made notes about each of them.

Bill, a supervisor in manufacturing, has been with the company nine years. Dorothy is also a manufacturing supervisor. She has been with the company for seven years and has recently transferred to the team from Marketing. Marcus is a packaging supervisor who is new with the company but had worked in manufacturing in his last job. Cecelia supervises the shipping and purchasing areas and has worked as a manufacturing supervisor for five years.

Chris runs the engineering function. He had spent three years with corporate engineering after completing his degree and has been with the team for one year. Jan supervises the accounting area and functions as controller for the team. She had worked in several other companies in the accounting and finance areas. She has been part of the team for five years.

When the introductions were finished, Jan the team's controller said, "I had asked the team to help me develop a solution to some budgeting snags that have arisen. Since that item is on our agenda I had already begun."

"Let's finish that discussion. Then I want the second item to be TMT time to refocus on team performance so our guest can leave if he chooses," the Manager responded.

The lively discussion that had been in progress resumed. Larry made several observations about the team's behavior which reinforced some of his reading about high performing teams.

- The individual members made most of their contributions by making statements rather than by asking questions.

- When questions were asked they were for clarification, or to seek more information, rather than to trap another team member.

- Each member was listened to by the rest of the team.

- The discussion was managed by Jan, who needed ideas from the team.

- When a disagreement occurred between two members, Jan stated that she had heard both points of view and would use them in her decision.

- Finally, she asked if there were other comments and when there were none, summarized what she had heard and thanked the group members for their help.

The Supervisor was amazed when several of the members thanked her for asking them to comment. He was even more amazed when he realized that all of the team members had contributed and that only a few minutes had passed. He could hardly wait to ask the Manager if some of his observations were accurate reflections of the team and if he had observed some of the ingredients of a high performing team. He also needed to know what Patricia meant by "TMT time."

*　*　*　*　*

"I've been thinking about your earlier question," she said, after they had returned to Patricia's office. "I want to talk about the elements of high performance. Leadership is important to any team, and is one of ten elements of a high performing team. The second critical element is purpose. My performance and the performance of my team will be judged by what we produce and how we are viewed by others outside the team. Therefore, as the manager I get the team to focus on both internal and external elements."

"Does that mean there are four elements which contribute to becoming a high performing team?" Larry asked.

"There are many elements which contribute to becoming a high performing team," chuckled the Manager, recognizing Larry's impatience. "I focus on four external elements and four internal elements. Let me outline them on the chalkboard."

The Manager drew the following diagram:

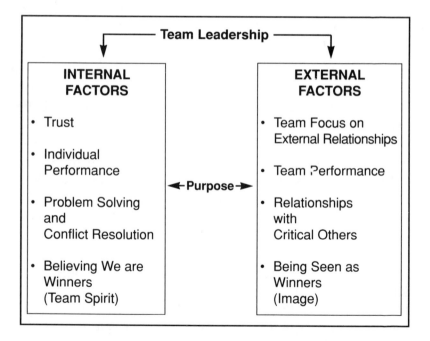

"To start, you could say that high performing teams must function well as a team (Internal) and they must also perform well with other teams, customers, and suppliers (External)," the Manager concluded after she finished the chart.

"That's a terrific notion!" exclaimed Larry as he rapidly made notes. He could begin to see some changes for his team: High performance requires leadership, purpose, an internal focus and an external focus. Within each focus are four critical elements. "If there are ten elements, how do you keep the team focused on all of them?" he asked.

"Before I answer you, I would like to ask you to do a small experiment. I want you to watch my left hand while we talk."

"Well, of course." he stammered. "What could she be up to?" he wondered.

"Remember the ten minute session at the team meeting?" she asked.

"What is 'TMT time'?" Larry asked, interrupting Patricia. Rather than replying, she continued, "The task in that session was to have us refocus on our team performance. I heard from the team members about how their teams were performing and how their teams could perform more effectively. Next week we will be using our ten minutes to focus on the purpose of the team.

"What have you observed about my left hand?" the Manager asked without warning.

"Well, I noticed that you pointed once, and that you picked up a pen, but that for the most part your left hand was resting on the desk," he responded.

"Excellent, and now what did you notice about my right hand?" the Manager asked.

"I didn't really notice your right hand," mumbled Larry, feeling a little set up.

"Don't feel badly," said the Manager. "The point of my experiment was just that. When your attention is focused on one task, other tasks tend to slip slightly out of focus. That is why we spend ten minutes every week focusing on a different element of team performance. All too often teams focus on one aspect of their work continuously, to the exclusion of other aspects. Therefore, one of the team leader's jobs is to regularly draw the team's attention to other important elements of high performance."

"I see your point," Larry interjected. "I really did focus on one hand to the exclusion of the other, merely as a result of your request. I can see how production targets could become the only focus. So how do you keep a team's focus on more than one element of performance?"

"First, by having a high performance model with which all team members are familiar, like the one I drew on the board. Second, by focusing on a different element for ten minutes each week we increase our awareness of that element. Within eight to ten weeks we have covered all of the elements and are back to refocus on the first one. This keeps all of them in some focus and also helps us to develop a perspective on where we need to improve.

"For instance if there had been lots of difficulty focusing on performance this week, and if we had had difficulty refocusing on performance the last time, that would be an indication that we need a longer session on performance and that I need to spend some individual time with team members."

"I think I understand what you mean," said Larry. "May I read what I've written down to be sure?"

- *High performing teams need competent leadership.*
- *High performing teams need clear purpose.*
- *High performing teams need both an internal and external focus.*
- *There are four elements which contribute to internal excellence; trust, individual performance, problem solving/conflict resolution, and team members believing they are winners.*
- *There are four elements which contribute to external excellence; identifying critical others, team performance, relationships with critical others, and being seen as winners.*
- *The leader's task is to help the team keep all of the elements in focus.*
- *Focus is maintained by regularly reviewing each element in a Ten Minute Team session.*
- *Finally, if the team has problems with an element in a review session, that is an indication that more attention needs to be paid to that element.*

"That is an excellent summary. Let's schedule time next week to talk about leadership and TMT time," suggested Patricia.

Step 1

LEADERSHIP OF HIGH PERFORMING TEAMS

As soon as he was inside Patricia's office Larry asked, "What is leadership on a high performing team?" "Before you examine the team you must look at the team leader," replied the Manager. "Team leaders play critical roles in developing high performing teams. While the individual leader's style and skills may vary, there is one attribute which must be present."

"What is it?" Larry interjected.

"Well, in addition to having some basic managerial skills the team leader must really believe in the value of teamwork. Too many managers pay lip service to teamwork and don't put any effort into developing the team. It seems obvious to me that if you believe the best way to achieve a goal is through individual effort then you won't be an effective team leader. And you certainly won't be able to develop a high performing team.

"My experiences with my work teams, my family and my women's soccer team all increase my belief that a high performing team leads to greater achievement and to greater individual satisfaction," said the Manager.

"How does a manager put effort into developing a team?" asked the Supervisor, looking puzzled.

"First, the team leader sets a climate where the importance of teamwork is stressed," replied the Manager. "I tell my team members that I expect them to work as a team. I have them discuss team goals. I give praise for team cooperation and I give reprimands for failure to cooperate or failure to consider the entire team. However, the most important thing I do is to provide opportunities for the team to focus on our performance as a team.

"At each team meeting I set aside ten minutes, referred to as Ten Minute Team time, or TMT time where we explicitly focus on one of the steps to building high performing teams. This time is so important that we call ourselves the *Ten Minute Team*."

"So that's what TMT time is," thought Larry. "Isn't that a little unusual?" he asked. "A Ten Minute Team sounds like a gimmick."

"It may be a gimmick, but it reinforces the point that if you choose you can develop a high performing team by spending ten minutes on a regular basis. The team leader must keep the team focused on the correct issues."

"Well I certainly can see how your behavior as the team leader is important to developing a high performing team, but 'Ten Minute Team' sounds like a gimmick—not a set of steps," stated the Supervisor. "I don't see how you can develop a team in only ten minutes. My work team spent three days with a consultant and even then we weren't a high performing team. And my last company had a class on team work and the instructor never suggested that teams could be developed so easily!" Larry protested.

Patricia looked Larry in the eye, placed her hand lightly on his arm and said, "If you want to learn about developing teams you must be more open to new ideas. I'm disappointed in you."

Larry was momentarily stunned, but then recognized the value of the observation. "I think you are right," he replied. "But time is so important to me."

"Time is important to all of us, especially managers, and that is why Ten Minute Team (TMT) sessions are so valuable," she replied. "My team doesn't meet often and when we do our meetings are short. On one hand, ten minutes is a large enough amount of time in our meetings to signify the importance of our team and, on the other hand, it is small enough for us to conduct other business. My role as team leader is to make sure that we keep a focus on the team in the same way that we focus on our work."

"I think I understand," said the Supervisor. "Let me summarize."

> - *The team leader must believe in teams.*
> - *The team leader must state expectations about teamwork and give praise and reprimands to support the expectations.*
> - *The team leader must set aside time in team meetings to focus on the team's performance and development.*

"I think you have it," said Patricia. "You listen well and your summary is brief and clear. I like that."

"What are the steps to building a high performing team then?" asked Larry, feeling good about himself after the praise.

"The answer to that question will be demonstrated more clearly if you can attend our next team meeting," said Patricia. "We are going to spend ten minutes refocusing on our purpose at that meeting."

"I'm flattered to be asked and I will be there," said the Supervisor, closing his note pad.

Step 2

PURPOSE

Larry arrived at Patricia's office a few minutes before the team meeting. He had been thinking about the phrase she had used, "refocusing on our purpose," and wanted to ask some questions about its meaning. As before, he was shown into her office without waiting. He apologized for arriving early and said he needed more clarity before the team meeting. Patricia seemed pleased at his interest.

"Today we are going to refocus on our purpose, but before you can refocus, the team has to have previously arrived at a purpose. To do this the manager must be clear on the purpose of the organization, and the purpose of the team in the organization," the Manager responded.

"Oh, where I work that is simple," said the Supervisor. "The purpose of the organization is to make money and the purpose of the team is to come in under budget."

"In some departments that may be true, but I think there are better ways to state purpose. While it is true that the purpose of a team is to support the purpose of the company, the manner in which that support is best given will vary," responded the Manager.

"Teams get in trouble because they frequently fail to see the appropriate link between their purpose and the organization's purpose. Suppose, as you suggested, the only purpose of the organization is to make money for the owners. Team leaders or department managers all too often interpret this as meaning they need to contribute to earnings by controlling costs. While this may be appropriate for some teams, there will be other teams which need to spend more to earn more.

"In any case if earnings is an organization's purpose the organization has made a poor choice. Earnings should be the result of fulfilling purpose."

"Is purpose like vision or mission?" Larry asked.

"Well, purpose could be seen as similar to mission in that it is a general statement about the reason the organization exists. However, purpose is more active and is both in the future and in the present," she responded.

"I'm not sure that I understand the difference," Larry said, looking confused.

"Vision tends to imply a future condition that an organization is attempting to achieve. An example is: To be the number one company in the industry in customer satisfaction," said the Manager. "This does provide you a goal statement which can guide your activities, but it is too far away to provide clear direction or feedback on your progress."

"I understand that," responded Larry. "One of our goals is to contribute to the security of the nation. I don't have any idea if my work makes any difference. How is purpose different?"

"One of the purpose statements of this company which affects my department is: Deliver a defect-free product to the customer. With that as a guideline I can institute quality measures and determine daily if my department's work is consistent with that company purpose," said the Manager.

"I can see where that would be helpful. I go for months not really knowing if my group is working toward the correct goal," said the Supervisor reflectively. "This is going to be more complicated than I thought. How do you get clear on purpose?"

"By applying ten minute time to purpose. I attempt to get clear on what I believe the purpose to be and then I have members of the team do the same thing on their own. Then we spend ten minutes in the team meeting developing a team purpose," the Manager replied.

Larry could hardly hide his disbelief. "You spent ten minutes developing a purpose statement!" he snorted. "Most teams spend weeks on that job."

"I know," Patricia replied. "That's why they're not high performing! Let's go to the meeting and maybe you will see and understand what I mean." "I need a minute to make some notes," said Larry. He quickly listed the following points.

- *Teams must be clear on how they support organization purpose.*
- *Purpose provides daily guidance as well as future goals.*
- *Individuals should be able to see the link between their work, their team's purpose and the organization's purpose.*
- *Teams need to refocus on purpose from time to time.*

*   *   *   *   *

"I asked all of you to think about our team's purpose and how you and your unit are contributing to that purpose. I also asked you to think about what each of you need to do differently to direct your total effort toward the team purpose. We will proceed in our normal TMT fashion, with each of you making a statement, followed by a brief discussion, followed by a summary from one of us. As usual I'll keep the time. Let's begin on my right and go around the table."

Each member made a brief statement about what her/his unit could to do to contribute more fully to the TMT's purpose. Each member also made a statement about what the TMT needed to do differently in order to more fully achieve its own purpose. As the members spoke, Larry was startled at the candidness with which each member discussed her/his unit and how they could improve. He was also struck by the similarity in the statements about the TMT and how it could improve. The statements centered around individual units needing to focus more on production targets and the TMT needing to focus more on accountability.

When the team member on Patricia's left finished, Patricia spoke about what she could do personally to refocus on the team's purpose and about what she thought the team needed to do differently. Her statement about the team echoed those of the team members. She ended by saying, "We have seven minutes left and I would like to reserve two of those for summarizing. Let's begin the discussion."

Most of the discussion centered on sharpening the work that needed to be done to keep individual unit efforts accountable to the TMT purpose, thereby helping to refocus the manager's team. In addition, Larry noticed that several members said that they agreed with other members' observations of their own teams. Most members offered suggestions to others, and some made concrete offers of assistance. In less than five minutes the discussion paused. After a few seconds of silence a younger man who had been less vocal than others said, "I think I have a summary."

He listed four points that had emerged from the the discussion. When he had finished there was a longer pause.

"Are there disagreements with Chris' summary?" Patricia asked.

One team member said that she agreed totally and thought that Chris had given an accurate summary. Several other team members voiced their agreement.

"I agree also," said the Manager. "If there is no further discussion, I want each of you to discuss our refocusing points with your units and to adjust your activities accordingly." She turned to Larry and said, "Larry, now that you have seen a TMT session do you have any questions?"

"I don't think so," he responded. "However, I would like to list the steps I saw in the Ten Minute team process and see if I have all of them."

- **Each team member knows the Ten Minute Team task before the meeting.**

- **Each team member is prepared.**

- **Each team member makes her/his contribution.**

- **The leader makes her/his comments last.**

- **Discussion occurs after everyone has made individual contributions.**

- **Someone summarizes, the summary is amended and accepted.**

Several of the team members expressed their agreement with the summary.

"I have to go to my own team meeting now, but would like to discuss this session and other TMT activities later," Larry said.

"You are welcome to call or visit any time," Patricia replied.

*   *   *   *   *

"Well, that was pretty impressive," Larry thought as he drove to work. The team had handled the refocusing more effectively than any other team, doing any task, he had ever witnessed. They reminded him of a professional football team doing a two minute drill. Maybe, that's where the idea of Ten Minute Team came from. He'd have to ask. But teams have to produce results. Maybe this team was just good at its processes. After all, while most football teams had two minute drills, not all of them actually scored in the last two minutes.

He would pursue these questions about team performance with the Manager the next time they met.

Larry was pleasantly surprised when Patricia called him at work the next morning. He was even more surprised when she asked for feedback on the meeting.

"What did you observe," she asked?

He mentioned the team's effective use of time, its ability to handle disagreements and to come to an agreement. "However, there is more to performance than process," he stated. "While your team is good at refocusing on its purpose, is it as good at completing its task?" "

I think so," replied the Manager, "but I'm biased. How would you like to talk to a Manager whose team works directly with mine?"

"That would be great."

"Fine, give me some times when you are available and I'll arrange a meeting for you," Patricia said.

Step 3

RELATIONSHIPS WITH CRITICAL OTHERS

It was a few days before the appointment was confirmed. Larry started with a visit to the Manager. As usual he was able to get right in to see her and visit for a few minutes.

"It's nearly time for your appointment with Mr. Garcia. His team relies on this department's output, so when we have problems, we create problems for him. In many ways he is our real customer. He is a good person to talk with about our performance. He is expecting you and has agreed to answer any of your questions. He has also agreed that you can discuss his comments with me. My secretary can tell you how to find his office."

As he was walking to the meeting, Larry mused about the meaning of high performing teams. All of the articles he had read focused on matters internal to the team, yet the Ten Minute Team Manager was having him talk to a manager outside the team. This particular manager, Mr. Garcia, could be very critical of the team since his own team was dependent on the Ten Minute Team. Larry was looking forward to his comments.

He was shown directly into Mr. Garcia's office. He was engaged in a forceful conversation on the phone. Without pause Mr. Garcia ended the conversation and pivoted his chair to face Larry.

"Well, so you're from the Ten Minute Team!" he exclaimed. Without waiting for an answer he continued,

"I haven't seen anyone from the TMT for at least a week. I've been wondering if they were still in business."

Larry realized that Mr. Garcia was kidding him but didn't understand why. "Well, I'm not really with the Ten Minute Team", he stammered, wanting to set Mr. Garcia straight. "I really work at the West Plant and I'm trying to understand the TMT. I want to develop a high performing team, and—"

"Whoa," interrupted Mr. Garcia, "I know all that—Pat briefed me last week. She calls me regularly to brief me on any project her team takes on which will impact me or my team. In fact, I have been expecting to see Cecelia, their shipping supervisor. She usually comes by for a meeting every week or so. I'm really impressed when another manager's subordinate feels free to come to me to get feedback on team performance. Well, what can I do for you?"

"I am learning about high performing teams and the Production Manager, Patricia, suggested that I interview you about her team," Larry responded.

"Well let me tell you, that bunch is a lot different than any other team I've ever worked with. They make more demands on me, and sometimes they irritate me, but they do perform!" Mr.Garcia responded.

"How do they irritate you?" Larry asked, in anticipation of finally seeing through the Ten Minute Team mystique.

"They irritate me because they make demands on me. They want to know how they can provide me with better service. They want to know what my schedule is for the next thirty days. They want to know if I have any new or different activities coming up. They ask about my expectations, the expectations of my people, problems with their team members, etc. In short, they make me think a lot more about how I manage and plan. Anyone who does that is an irritant," he said reflectively.

After a brief pause he continued, "Now don't get me wrong, the interactions I have with the Ten Minute Team make me a better manager. Even though they irritate me sometimes, I'm really glad they exist. You can tell them that if you want. I haven't but I should."

Mr. Garcia's last comments were not what Larry had anticipated. Thinking that maybe he had asked the wrong question he said, "I don't think irritating you contributes to the Ten Minute Team's performance. What do you think?"

Mr. Garcia's first response was the look of disbelief he gave to Larry. "What did you say your job is?" he asked.

"I'm a new production supervisor at the West Plant," Larry responded, realizing he was about to get a lecture.

"Let me tell you something," said Garcia, leaning forward. "All those questions do several things which contribute to the Ten Minute Team's performance. First, I get to know them and they get to know me. That's important. Second, they know exactly what I expect from them and what their targets should be. Third, if they are going to have trouble with my expectations they can discuss them with me before I do the schedule rather than after they are behind. Fourth, the conversations we have help me to plan better, and if I plan better then they have an easier time doing their job. Finally, they treat me like a valuable team member so that we work together rather than me hassling them; which is how most teams operate with each other."

A long pause followed while Larry made notes. Finally, he looked up and said, "I think I understand the impact of communication with people outside your team on your own team's performance a lot better. You have been very helpful."

With a trace of a smile Mr. Garcia acknowledged the comment and said, "Call me anytime. I have lots to say to new supervisors that you won't learn in training programs." With that he rose, and extended his hand.

That evening as he was reviewing his notes Larry began to suspect that the interaction between the Ten Minute Team and Mr. Garcia wasn't all by accident. He realized that there were several questions he wanted to ask Patricia. He telephoned her the following morning.

"How did you like Mr.Garcia?" Patricia asked as soon as she had greeted him.

"He was pretty direct, and he really likes your team," Larry replied.

"Yes, he is direct, I like that," she replied. "Now tell me what you learned about high performing teams as a result of your visit with Mr. Garcia."

"I thought you might ask that," Larry said with a trace of humor in his voice. "So I made some notes last night. Let me list how I think your team improves its performance through your communication with Mr. Garcia."

- *You clarify the other person's performance expectations of your team.*

- *You get current feedback about your team's performance.*

- *You maintain a positive relationship with a critical person in the organization.*

- *You strengthen your team by having one of your subordinates be the primary link between you and the other manager.*

- *Finally, you help the other manager improve her/his own team's performance, which helps everyone.*

"That is a very interesting summary," said Patricia thoughtfully. "I don't believe I've ever seen the benefits as clearly. I think we are both going to learn from your project."

"Maybe you can answer some questions for me as well," he replied. "I suspect the interactions you and your team have with Mr. Garcia aren't by accident, and if I'm correct I'd like to know how you decide what to do with other teams in the organization."

Step 4

TEAM FOCUS ON EXTERNAL RELATIONSHIPS

"You are correct in your suspicion," the Manager responded. "We actively and consciously work to maintain excellent relationships with numerous individuals and groups in the organization who are critical to our success. And we use Ten Minute Team time to guide us."

"How do you maintain excellent external relationships with a Ten Minute Team activity?" interrupted Larry. "The other people aren't even in the room."

"Of course they are not in the room," the Manager replied with just a hint of impatience in her voice. "But we use the ten minutes to clarify who the critical others are and how we are working with them. Let me be more specific and describe how we focused on external relationships recently.

"We always begin by quickly reviewing our list of critical others. The list has evolved over time. I ask if there are any changes to the list, new critical others, or ones who are no longer critical. As you might imagine in a fairly stable organization, the list doesn't change all that often. If your team doesn't have a list of critical others you should get the team to make the list at your next meeting.

"We have also ranked the critical others in terms of how much they influence our success in the organization. The ranking doesn't change very much either.

However, we had lots of arguments arriving at the first ranking.

"After the review of the list, usually not more than a minute, I ask for a credibility check. The credibility check is our way of sharing how we see our credibility with each of the critical others. The credibility level will change with events in the organization. If we believe that credibility is slipping, then we have identified a target for relationship building."

"I think I know how you determine a change in the credibility level," interrupted Larry with a laugh. "You send a team member, or a visiting supervisor, to meet with one of the critical others to see how your team is doing."

"That is certainly one way to assess credibility and we do use it regularly," replied the Manager. "We also use other techniques. For example, in a ten minute session after we have reviewed the list of critical others, I will ask for headlines regarding any recent incidents of which team members are aware, which may have impacted our credibility. If the headline activity produces items which may have negative impacts, we will add an agenda item. The agenda item will cause us to focus on a strategy and action steps for rebuilding our credibility."

"Who determines the strategy and action steps? And, who works on rebuilding the credibility?" asked Larry.

"The team will briefly review the incident and then we will decide who should work with the critical other. That person will then have no more than five minutes to get suggestions, cautions and advice from other team members. I will then spend time, if requested, with that team member to discuss strategy and action steps. Occasionally, I am the appropriate person to contact the critical other, but if possible I leave it to the team member who normally interacts with that person or group," the Manager said.

"I see how using all the team members is a good idea," said Larry. "In my team I am the one who deals with all outsiders. Sometimes, I don't know what is needed as well as one of my people. It also takes lots of my time."

"It also takes opportunities to learn and to get exposure away from your staff!" replied Patricia emphatically. "This is one key difference between traditional and high performing teams."

"This is all very useful," said Larry. "I have two more questions, if you have the time." Without waiting for an answer he continued. "Are there other techniques that you use, and does focusing on others outside of the team really help?"

"One other technique we employ is to quickly identify current hot spots, or areas which may change in the near future which could affect our team. This allows us to anticipate requests or problems before they come to us," responded the Manager.

"In reply to your second question, of course this really works! In my experience, all high performing teams have excellent intelligence about their environments. The military uses spies, scouts and informers. Athletic teams scout their opponents, and good managers stay plugged into the organization's grapevine. We just apply a more open and positive strategy.

"We focus on the needs and opinions of critical others in our organization, and we go directly to them to seek information about our performance and how to improve that performance. We see them as critical to our success and as our collaborators in pursuing the organization's purpose.

"For example, a few months ago Mr. Garcia had a high visibility rush order. During that time he became the most critical person in the organization for us. If his order had been delayed because of us we would have been in trouble. Cecelia found out about the order the same day Mr. Garcia got it. She talked to me. We moved Mr. Garcia's work up in priority and Cecelia put more attention on his needs. We purchased the raw materials and scheduled shipping accordingly. As a result we provided him with our part of the order early and increased our credibility."

After a pause, while he made notes, Larry replied, "I am learning a lot about high performing teams. I think I am going to be a better supervisor as a result of our talks. I would like to summarize what you have just said."

- *The team develops a list of critical others.*
- *The team regularly looks for additions, changes, deletions to the list.*
- *Recent events which may change the team's credibility are headlined.*
- *An individual is identified to work with each critical other.*
- *The team provides advice to that individual.*
- *If asked, the manager assists with strategy and action steps.*

"That is a good description of the Ten Minute Team activity for identifying and maintaining critical external relationships," said the Manager.

"There is a lot to becoming a high performing team," said Larry. "It seems that each time we talk I learn about another element. I want to know about the others."

Step 5

TRUST

"There are several more elements which I listed at our last meeting that are important," replied the Manager. "For example, at our next staff meeting we are going to focus on the most important internal element of a high performing team—trust."

"I would really like to observe that session!" exclaimed Larry. "Several of the articles I have been reading say that trust is the most important element in team performance. However, there isn't much information about how you actually develop trust. I've always thought that trust took years to develop, and since most teams aren't together for years, maybe having trust in a work team is too high an expectation."

The Manager hesitated a minute and then said with conviction, "I believe that trust can be developed rapidly and maintained, but that the team leader and the team have to actively focus on trust building rather than hoping that trust occurs as a result of time and experience. I would like for you to attend our next staff meeting and then to share your reactions with the team."

The staff meeting was just beginning when Larry arrived. Several of the staff members greeted him with words and smiles. Even though this was only his second meeting with the team, he was pleased to join them.

"We have been reviewing the agenda for today," the Manager said, "and we are about to spend ten minutes refocusing on trust. We will begin, as we usually do, with each one of us making statements, followed by discussion and a summary."

The Manager turned to Chris, from Engineering, who was seated next to her and asked if he would begin. Larry noted that this was the quiet team member who had summarized the last meeting. As each member spoke Larry wrote down some of the comments.

"My trust of Bill was shaken when I heard from someone in the cafeteria that he was discussing my project."

"I realized my trust of the entire team was justified when we finished the last project on schedule."

"My trust of Cecelia went up last week when she told me that I was letting her down with my performance."

"I trust this team totally and that hasn't been impacted by any recent events."

"My trust for the Manager will be impacted negatively if we do not have my review when it is scheduled next week."

As the statements were made Larry could actually see the team members relax and draw closer to each other even though there was a table between them. He was very surprised that even mentioning incidents where trust may have been harmed seemed to have a positive impact on the team. When all of the team members had spoken there was a brief pause. Bill, the manufacturing supervisor, then turned to Chris, who had made the statement about the cafeteria comments, and said, "I was talking about your project and I'm sorry if it impacted your trust in me. I would like to discuss this further after the staff meeting."

"I would like that also," Chris responded.

The Manager turned to Dorothy, the other manufacturing supervisor, and said, "I can assure you that I have your review in my calendar and am looking forward to meeting with you." She then turned to Larry and asked, "Larry, what experiences have you had recently which have impacted your trust levels with me or other members of this team?"

"Well, eh, I, eh, well I'm not sure," he stammered. "I don't know if this fits but I think that I have learned to trust you more because you have been open with me when I've asked questions. And I liked it last week when I heard you say that you might learn from me. I think that comment, for some reason, made me trust you more. And one other thing, I thought you were taking a big risk sending me to talk to Mr. Garcia about this group's performance. So when you took that risk by trusting me, I felt more trust in you. And I don't know how to say this but, well, you have been nice to me, and I think that helps me to trust you. Actually the entire team has been open with me, taken risks in my presence, shown interest in my project, been vulnerable in my presence, and provided support to me." Feeling slightly embarrassed and unsure if he was making any sense Larry paused and looked around. The team members were smiling at him.

The Manager looked him in the eye and said, "Has this last minute impacted your trust for me or this team?"

"Why yes it has," he responded reflectively. "I was open with my thoughts, which was taking a risk for me, and you all seemed supportive of me, and no one laughed or made me feel foolish. I also feel more like a team member because I did what others were doing. Yes, I believe my trust of this team just went up."

"Can you tell us what you have learned about trust from the last few minutes?" asked the Manager.

"I think so," said Larry. "Let me organize my notes for a minute then I'll try to summarize."

- *Trust is built by focusing directly on it.*
- *Taking risks is necessary to build trust.*
- *Getting supported for taking risks builds trust.*
- *Allowing yourself to be vulnerable increases others' trust of you.*
- *Caring about each other is necessary to establish trust.*
- *Letting go of negative incidents in the past is critical to trust building.*

"Did I miss anything?" asked Larry. The team assured him that they agreed with his summary, and had found it useful to help them sharpen their own definitions.

Larry sat through the rest of the staff meeting and once again was impressed with the speed and thoroughness with which the team completed its tasks. He couldn't think of another team where the communication was so effective. He decided to ask Patricia about communication after the meeting. He couldn't remember her ever mentioning it as one of the keys to high performance, even though it appeared in several articles as a key element.

After the meeting as they were walking to the Manager's office Larry raised his question about communication. Patricia's answer was quick and decisive.

"Communication is the result of high trust!" she stated.

When she didn't elaborate, Larry said, "Yes, but isn't communication also good listening skills, and good speaking ability, and courtesy, and assertiveness and knowing what you are talking about?"

"Of course, all of those are aids to effective communication," Patricia replied. "However without trust, good listeners don't listen, effective speakers don't speak and assertive speakers argue with other assertive speakers! I can take a team of people without the skills you mentioned and if they trust each other they will communicate excellently as a team. We can learn the skills, and we can help each other in technical areas. Without trust, however, the team will at best remain mediocre."

"You sound irritated with communication," observed Larry.

"I'm irritated because so much time and energy gets spent attempting to improve communication and blaming poor performance on communication, when I believe the cause is trust. Improving communication is a worthwhile activity, but poor communication is a symptom of poor performance and low trust—not the cause!" she stated emphatically.

"I think I agree, but I need some more time to reflect on this," said Larry. He was already reflecting on the amount of time and money invested, and the training his team had received in communication skills. He was also contrasting the TMT meeting with frequent examples of poor communication he had witnessed recently.

"Do you have any other techniques you use to improve trust," he asked?

"We have used several activities that have helped," responded the Manager. "For example, we check to see if members have irritations they are holding onto that they can let go of. If there are any, the team member says, 'I'm going to let go of this issue' and names the issue. Team members have also gone around the table and identified the individuals they felt the most or least trust for and discussed the reasons. Where trust was low, members paired and met after the meeting to build trust."

"You have done more than any team I know to consciously build trust!" exclaimed Larry. "I would like to put my notes together and then come back next week, if that is OK, to learn more."

"Please call when you are ready," the Manager responded.

Step 6

INDIVIDUAL PERFORMANCE

The past few weeks had been very satisfying for Larry. He was progressing nicely in his new job and he was enjoying his contact with Patricia and the Ten Minute Team. He had started referring to them as the TMT in all of his notes and discussions. The best thing about the project was that he was learning lots about team leadership as well as about team performance. As he reflected on the TMT, he couldn't help but compare them to his own team. His team just didn't have the same spirit and, as near as he could tell, didn't perform as well. He wondered if the high performing Manager had just been smart, or lucky, in selecting the team members. Maybe the secret to high performing teams was really selecting high performing individuals.

He reflected on his own experience as a team member and now as a team supervisor. He had been near the top of his engineering undergraduate class and had received a high salary offer. His first engineering work group had been composed of seven other engineers with similar credentials. His memory of that team was one of bickering, missed deadlines and lectures from the engineering manager about his experiences with the Army Corps of Engineers.

His current team was a little better, after all, he was the supervisor. But it never seemed to perform up to his expectations. He wondered if it was because of his leadership, or was it the quality of his team members, or was it because his team wasn't really a team? He decided that maybe Patricia would be a good person to talk to about these questions, when he met with her the next day.

The secretary informed Larry that Patricia was still meeting with Dorothy but as soon as that meeting ended the Manager could see him. A few minutes later Dorothy and Patricia emerged from the office laughing, and looking pleased with themselves. Larry wondered what jokes women told when men weren't around.

When he was seated in the Manager's office, he commented about the laughter and asked what the joke was about. Patricia looked puzzled and then replied, "Oh, there was no joke. We had just completed Dorothy's performance review and were reflecting on how pleasant this meeting was compared to our first review a year ago."

"Well I've certainly never had much to laugh about after my performance reviews, even though they have always been pretty good," Larry asserted, feeling a little off balance about the Manager's response. "I actually wanted to talk to you today about performance. Is outstanding team performance the result of outstanding individuals or the result of outstanding individual performance?"

"I don't think it's either of those," Patricia said, after a moment's pause. "I think outstanding team performance is just that—outstanding team performance. My team members are all great as people, but not one of them is the most talented person in the organization in their specialty. In fact, two of them were viewed as poor performers by their last manager.

"I believe this team performs as well as it does because each individual does a good job, and as a team we perform better than the sum of the individual contributions."

Her comments were too abstract for Larry to make notes about but he knew intuitively what she meant. He decided to pursue his questions about individual performance. "How do you work to improve individual performance?" he asked.

"I do what any other good manager should do," she responded. "One of the differences, however, is that *I do it.* I set individual performance goals with each of my team members. I give praise and I give reprimands when they are appropriate. I never let a review or counseling meeting with a team member go beyond when it is scheduled. I talk openly about development with my team and see that they work on their development. If a team member needs to improve skills and a training program is the answer, I see that s/he gets to that program. If coaching and on-job training are the answers, I work with that person to develop a plan which involves both our schedules.

"Most managers know what to do to improve an individual's skills, they just fail to do it. I have a peer in this organization who is always moaning about his team. He continually hopes to hire the right person who will save them. He is like a losing coach hoping to get a first round draft pick who will perform as well on the job as s/he did in college. My experience suggests that you hire the best people you can find. You actively work to integrate them into the team and then help them develop the skills they need to perform to the best of their ability," she continued.

"That certainly fits my experience," sighed Larry. "My past managers rarely talked to me about what I needed to do to improve my performance. They talked about my past performance, and sometimes I felt that they didn't want me to perform better. I have been wanting to attend a strategic management course for a year. My current manager just asks, 'Why would anyone want to attend a course like that?'"

"You said a few minutes ago that individual performance isn't the explanation for team performance. Could you say more about that?" he asked.

"One thing I learned playing competitive soccer," replied Patricia, "is that in the long run, a team is only as good as its weakest member. In the short term, teams can always cover for the weak member, but not for the long term. If you watch most teams you will see the highest performers get the rewards, recognition and promotions. They also tend to get most of the positive emotional support from the team. They get the interesting assignments, and as a rule get more time with their supervisor. It is no wonder then, that they are high performers.

"The low performers, on the other hand, get few or none of the rewards, recognition or promotions. The emotional support they get is usually negative, or at best sympathy for doing a poor job. Think about how limiting it is to be told, 'Oh well, you did your best,' when everyone knows that it was a poor effort. Where is the incentive and support to do better?" she asked, rhetorically.

"Well, yes, I see your point and I have also seen the stars get the rewards while the rest of us get left out. But, I'm still not sure what to do, or how this impacts team performance," Larry asked, looking puzzled.

"In a high performing team each member has to do her or his job effectively," began the Manager. "In addition each team member has to cover any uncovered base. If they see part of the team's work not being done, they have to take responsibility for seeing that it gets done. Finally, each team member has to take responsibility for the welfare of other team members. Because, as I said earlier, the team is only as good as the lowest performing team member.

"I don't believe that teams are saved by top draft choices. It is unrealistic in most organizations to believe that you will have access to the very best potential performer for each of your jobs. And it is unrealistic to believe that even if you could pick the top potential performers, that they would automatically perform up to their potential or that they could become a member of a team. The team has to work with each member to help that member perform to his or her potential!" Patricia stated emphatically.

"But how do you, as Manager or as team member, help the low performer to improve?" asked Larry. "I mean how, specifically, do you do it?"

"My job is to get the other team members to do most of it," replied Patricia. "I can work with the individual to develop and to improve skills. But the magic which occurs when a team is performing at its peak depends on all the team members pulling together. So I stress that we as a team are all dependent on one another, and that I expect team members to work to support one another for the good of the team. I give praise to individuals who assist other team members, and I give praise to team members who ask for assistance.

"On the other hand I will <u>not</u> tolerate divisive behavior. I will <u>not</u> join in gossip about other team members. I will <u>not</u> allow one team member to put his or her interest ahead of another, which is one way of beginning to sacrifice the team for the individual's goals.

"I make it clear to the team members that I have high expectations for us as a team and for each of them as team members. I also make it clear that an individual failure is a team failure," Patricia said.

"I see what you do to encourage the team members to support each other. But what do team members actually do to support one another?" asked Larry.

"When someone is having difficulty they will usually ask for assistance. This often occurs at a team meeting. As you observed a few days ago when Jan, our controller, asked for assistance she got lots of ideas, and other team members were pleased to help," responded the Manager. "Sometimes they ask for assistance privately, as Dorothy did today in her performance review meeting."

"But didn't Jan have to have lots of confidence to ask for help in public, especially with you there?" he asked.

"Jan has gained confidence because of something else that team members do for each other," the Manager replied. "Members of this team really care about one another, and they recognize that everyone will have difficulties from time to time. So when someone has trouble, the first thing team members do is to let that person know that while they are concerned about performance, they also care about the person and would like to help.

"If a stranger fell down in an intersection, you would help her/him up, even though you don't have anything to gain from that. However all too often in work teams, when someone stumbles, the other team members pretend that they don't see, or that it isn't their business, or even worse they begin to complain and act punitively toward that team member. Without exception this behavior leads to lower individual performance, less team trust and therefore lower team performance," Patricia concluded.

"Yes, I have seen that," said Larry. "It sounds like when a team member's performance is lagging that is the time they should get praise and support, which is counter to what we tend to do. We reward when people are succeeding, which is fine, but we ignore or punish when people are failing, which doesn't really make sense."

"You are absolutely right," said Patricia, with a smile. "On this team when someone is not performing as well as they are capable, or when they are having personal problems, the entire team rallies around them with support, advice and extra effort to assist that person to regain her/his performance level. Each of us believes that the other team members have the ability to be outstanding performers, and part of each of our individual jobs is to help other team members perform up to her/his potential."

"It all seems pretty simple," mused Larry. "I wonder why other teams are not performing up to their potential?"

"I can't answer for other teams," replied Patricia. "But I can answer for this team. One of the reasons we have individual high performance is because I expect it and other team members desire it. You noticed Dorothy coming out of my office as you arrived. At our last team meeting she requested a performance appraisal. Dorothy is having performance problems. Her unit has missed its production target for the past two weeks and it looks like they will have trouble meeting it this week. I discussed goal setting, expectation setting with subordinates and unit teamwork with her."

"Those all sound like good topics," said Larry. "Are there other techniques that you use with your subordinates?"

"As I've mentioned before, I talk about the importance of performance with each person. I also provide clear statements about team goals and direction. This allows each individual to fit his/her unit's goals closely with the team's," said the Manager. "I also keep the team informed about the organization's goals. This way we stay aligned with the organization.

"However, as in Dorothy's case, I can only offer a few resources to help her improve her unit's performance. Her teammates can offer many other resources."

"How do they actually do that?" asked Larry. "I know when some of my peers are in trouble but I'm not sure how I could assist them, and they rarely ask for help."

"There are several activities I have developed over the years to get team members to assist each other," replied the Manager. "For example, I regularly ask each team member to identify three accomplishments they have planned for the next two months. I then have other team members identify ways in which they can assist each other in those accomplishments. Team members also publicly congratulate each other when any of them has accomplished something. Getting a reward for high performance seems to stimulate more high performance. It's important to celebrate the small victories."

"That all sounds exciting, and I can see how both your efforts and the efforts of other team members might stimulate higher individual performance," said Larry.

"Why don't you come to our production scheduling meeting this week and see," suggested the Manager.

*   *   *   *   *

The team members were already involved in a discussion when Patricia and Larry arrived for the scheduling meeting. When a pause occurred, Patricia stated that the purpose of the meeting was to review the past month's production numbers and to develop a schedule for the coming month. The team members began the review of the past month's staffing, production targets and line problems. After a few minutes there was a pause. Marcus, the packaging supervisor, broke the silence by saying to Dorothy:

"I am hesitant to bring this up, but I am concerned about your unit missing production targets. My team had slack time the last two weeks waiting for product and we're afraid it is going to happen again this week. I am concerned that our entire team keep production up, so if I can help I would like to but I need to know your plans."

Several other team members nodded in agreement. Dorothy slumped in her chair and sighed. After a minute she looked around the room and said, "I feel terrible about missing targets and letting the rest of you down. I spoke with Pat last week and am working on better goal setting and on setting expectations with my unit. But they are all so new! I'm not sure what else to do, or what will make the difference. Does anyone have any suggestions?"

"I used to work in your area," Bill responded. "Maybe I could meet with you after this meeting for a few minutes."

"Several of my team members were in that area before, maybe some of them could be rotated back," said Cecelia.

"I don't know much about your area, but I would be happy to just have lunch and talk about how you are doing," responded Jan, the controller.

"Well, since I opened up the subject," said Marcus, "my team and I talked about how we could help out in your area if you are behind and we are slack, but I wasn't sure that I should just butt in until I was asked."

After a brief pause Patricia said, "Dorothy, why don't you be responsible for taking action on these suggestions at the end of this meeting." She looked around the table, pausing for a moment with each person, then said, "I want each of you to know how pleased I am with you for joining Dorothy and me in solving a team problem. Now let's finish reviewing last month's performance."

At the end of the meeting Patricia turned to Larry and said, "I wonder if you have any comments for us about this meeting?"

"Well I think I understand a lot about getting the best performance from individuals and how team members can take responsibility for helping to improve individual performance," he said.

- *It is unrealistic to expect to hire top performers for all of your jobs.*

- *The manager must reward teamwork and eliminate divisive behavior.*

- *Coaching and training are made available for each team member.*

- *Team members must see a problem of one member as a problem for the entire team, and therefore as their own problem.*

- *Someone publicly informs the entire team about a performance problem that needs attention.*

- *The team member with the performance problem discusses the concerns s/he has.*

- *Members offer resources, ideas and support which might help.*

- *Finally, the team member with the problem takes responsibility for utilizing the resources offered.*

The Manager looked at Larry and said, "You are becoming a resource to this team and I value your observations, thank you."

As they walked back to Patricia's office Larry asked about employees, who at their best are not able to perform adequately in their job.

"What happens when you have gone through all of the steps with an employee and they still fail to perform at an acceptable level? I'm sure there are some people who just won't be able to satisfactorily perform in their job."

"In those cases the person must find a new job." responded the Manager.

"You mean you would fire them!" exclaimed Larry in surprise.

"Yes I might fire the person. But I wouldn't do that without first attempting to help the person improve her/his performance," responded Patricia, with a smile. "However, there are times when the person and the job do not match. In those cases the only solution for the person, and for the team, is to find another job. In this company, if I believed that a person could not do the job, even with the team's support, I would send the person to our personnel group for career counseling. They would look for another job within the company, and if there were none available then the person would be given notice. However, unacceptable performance has to be the reason for the termination."

"That sounds realistic," responded Larry. "But I prefer the idea that low performers can be helped to improve through their efforts and the support of their team."

That evening as he was reviewing his notes, he realized that even though all of his time with the Manager and Ten Minute Team had been focused on elements of a high performing team that he had never really asked the Manager how she stimulated high team performance directly.

"Maybe high level team performance is a result of lots of individual effort and comes through trust building and better problem solving," he thought. "But maybe there are some direct ways of moving a team toward high performance." He decided that the next question for the Manager would be about total team performance.

Step 7

TEAM PERFORMANCE

It was several weeks before Larry found enough free time from his own job to call the TMT Manager to resume his conversation. During that time he had experimented with several of the concepts he had learned from the TMT. To his surprise his own team had responded almost like the members of the TMT. When he discussed his reasons and goals, all of his team members were supportive. Even more to his surprise they had lots of ideas of their own about how the team's performance could be improved.

Patricia greeted him warmly on the phone and said she had been thinking about his last question: 'How do you manage an entire team to develop high performance?' She said that in thinking about the question she had become clearer herself and would like to discuss her thoughts. They agreed to meet the next day.

"You do lots of things to get high performance. You rehearse, you play together, you rotate jobs and you even breathe together," said the Manager.

"That sounds like lots of effort and togetherness," Larry commented. "I don't think I really understand what you mean, even though I'm sure there are lots of sound ideas in what you are saying. What do you mean by rehearse?"

"I mean exactly what the word implies," replied the Manager. "Practice for upcoming events in a simulated situation. The best analogy is what happens with an athletic team, or a performing artist. They rehearse and practice several times for each actual performance. Even in amateur performances you can readily tell the difference between those who have practiced and those who have not. In organizations it is even clearer. The unrehearsed team is a major drain on productivity.

"To begin with, most managers think that if they have all of the positions filled they have a team. Then they believe that since they have all the positions filled that the team can handle anything which arises. For the most part they fall short of the mark."

"I can agree with that, but what do you actually do to rehearse?" asked Larry.

"First we identify all the presentations, change projects, potential problem areas, and critical meetings that we can," replied the Manager. "We actively scan our future environment. If we get caught by an unexpected event, I am disappointed. Once we identify an event, we identify the principle team members, they take some time on their own to shape a scenario to respond. Then they present the scenario at a full team meeting."

"But we do that," said Larry. "We are always preparing for important presentations, we go over some presentations several times. We decide on who will say what and we discuss timing."

"That's a first step," responded the Manager. "Many teams do what you are describing. However, they often never actually do the presentation, they only argue about each other's potential part. We actually do the presentation and then discuss it.

"Almost every time, we discover that when the presentation is actually conducted it goes differently than we thought it would. The other difference is that when the team members rehearse together they develop a synergy and can build on and support each other. They really look like a team then and the presentation appears more whole than when the pieces have been prepared individually. This helps us to look like winners, which is another component of a high performing team. We should talk about *winning* soon."

"I think I understand what you are saying," replied Larry. "I can see how you take an extra step or two, when compared to my team. Tell me what you meant about playing together."

"Again, I mean basically what I said. We play together. We have gone to a Ropes course to test our ability to overcome physical tests as individuals and as a team. We even went to a short Outward Bound course. In both of these cases we were able to see areas where we needed to develop as a team. We always see the play as a means to strengthen the team. We will analyze the experience to see what we have learned and how the learnings apply to the work experience," said Patricia.

"Some of the best team development comes from just having fun together. We do learn about ourselves as a team but I think the fun and the camaraderie is what really makes us a stronger team. It is one thing to have a theoretical model of a team and to understand team concepts. It is entirely different to have a team that actually *feels* like a team. Team members like one another and feel proud to be part of the team. You know, we really feel like a family.

That feeling holds us together when the times get tough. Individual team members care for one another and will go the extra distance for each other and for the team."

After a pause Larry said, "I think being a member of the Ten Minute Team is different than being a member of my team. I am jealous. But not all teams can go to courses as a team."

"That's true," said the Manager. "But there are other ways to develop as a team. Most organizations offer courses, or have staff people who will assist a team if they really want to improve their performance. Sometimes we can't do things as a team. We send individual members to training. But, we get something out of that also.

"Many of my colleagues have their staff members report on their outside training experience. But I ask my team members to select a part of their experience that would strengthen us as a team and actually teach us. That strengthens the team member's learning and always assists the team. We really learn to appreciate one another's ability through this process."

"I see lots of possibilities for my team in this idea," said Larry. "I am aware of the difference in the way my work team performs and the way the team I am part of in the company softball league performs and feels! I like the softball team better, but I have never associated it with the fact that we are playing and not working. I'm really excited, because if my work could be more like my play I would enjoy work a lot more! I know I could be more productive. Do you do any other tips in this area?"

"We have some social events as a team," replied Patricia. "I know that many managers disagree with work associates spending social time together. I believe that some social contact is desirable. I encourage family and significant others to attend as well. After all, we are part of social systems as well as work systems. To this extent I believe that the members of each system should know each other well enough to understand the conflicting demands placed on the individual who is a member of both systems. The more we know about other team members the easier it is to function together."

"I agree," said Larry. "I feel better about the people in my team with whom I've had more contact. I trust them more and when they need something at work I respond more readily. I'm glad to hear your comments. You mentioned rotating jobs earlier. What did you mean?"

"Job rotation is just one of the standard approaches to team development which we practice," said the Manager. "Remember the meeting where team members were consulting with Dorothy? There were several offers of assistance because one of my staff and some of their unit members had worked in Dorothy's area. I encourage my immediate team members to rotate jobs as soon as they have fully mastered their current job. This usually occurs after a year to eighteen months. I also encourage them to rotate their unit members within their units and between the units. I am fully committed to seeing everyone become multiskilled."

"We do some job rotation at my plant," Larry responded thoughtfully. "But there isn't really lots of support for it. Once a manager gets a good team s/he wants to keep the team intact. And, often team members don't want to leave their friends."

"Those are both reasons why people do not wish to rotate," responded Patricia. "However, there are lots of organizational reasons why they should rotate. First, we have seen a huge increase in understanding and appreciation for each other's jobs. Once you really know what another person does you have a far greater appreciation for that person. The second benefit is that the individual develops more skills and as a result his/her value to the organization increases. We have seen many of our workers selected as supervisors for other departments. Where I find the most practical value in having supervisors and workers cross trained is that we never have problems covering when some- one is on vacation or is ill. There are individuals who can do the job and there are other individuals who are eager to learn the job."

"I certainly agree with all of your reasons. At the West Plant, even though we don't formally rotate peo- ple, you have to have your ticket punched in several areas to get the next promotion. It also seems like the people who have been in only one area never move," replied Larry. "I think I'd better look at my own career planning."

"I won't comment on West, but it certainly helps here. In addition, each time an employee broadens her/his skills or gains a better understanding of another employee's job, the team is strengthened. Not only my team, but the total company team gains," said Patricia with a smile.

"Everything you have said makes sense for develop- ing a high performing team," said Larry. "However, I really don't have a clue what you meant when you said that sometimes you breathed together! Were you kid- ding me, or do you really breathe together?"

"I'm surprised you think I would kid you," Patricia responded, with a grin. "Haven't I been straightforward with you so far?"

"Well, yes," stammered Larry. "But this sounds a little far fetched. And, it sounded like something a far-out consultant would say. You seem very stable and...well, regular. What do you mean?"

After a brief pause Patricia responded with a chuckle, "You aren't the only one who is skeptical. Some of my own staff were skeptical. However, when we looked at high performing teams in other companies and at athletic teams who are consistent high performers we discovered that they have a characteristic which can't be accounted for with logical analysis.

"These teams are more than the sum of individual talents and effective processes. They have an additional dimension. Some of the teams talked about it as a feeling, others talked of spirit, and still others talked about losing their individual identity and feeling like part of the larger team. I experienced a similar feeling when my soccer team was playing well, and when my work team is really working as a team."

"I know that feeling with my softball team, but I never believed that you could get that experience with a group of engineers," said Larry.

"Those engineers, or machinists, or secretaries are the same people who are on your softball team," retorted Patricia. "The difference is in the setting and the notion of team, not in the people. The question organizations need to answer is how do they instill that something extra which occurs with sports teams?

"That something extra is called *team spirit*. It comes from a group of individuals accomplishing something out of the ordinary, which no subgroup of them could have done without the contribution of all of the other members. At that moment they go beyond being a collection of individuals and for that moment become a high performing team.

"There are numerous way to improve a team's chances of becoming high performing and breathing together is one of them. More traditional methods include prayer, singing company songs and the pregame huddle. All of these activities cause team members to identify with each other in a nonrational way. For that moment they acknowledge that they are more than just parts of a well-trained unit. They are spiritually linked. It isn't by accident that almost everyone accepts team spirit as real and desirable. We only get skeptical when someone suggests the method for encouraging it, like breathing in unison."

"Well, I'm still skeptical, but at least I understand what you're talking about," said Larry. "Maybe you could let me know when you and the team are going to breathe together." He couldn't help but smile even as he said the words.

On his way to work Larry reviewed the points Patricia had made regarding developing a high performing team. He realized that although he did some of the activities with his team, there were several he had never thought about. The list included the following:

- *High performing teams anticipate important events.*

- *They rehearse, as a team, for the event.*

- *They play and learn together, i.e., a Ropes course or a supervisory skills course.*

- *Team members teach the rest of the team skills they acquire through training.*

- *Social activities as a team benefit the team.*

- *Job rotation and cross training help the team to perform at a higher level.*

- *High performing teams use nonrational methods to develop team spirit: breathing in unison, songs and pregame huddles.*

"I think this project is almost complete," thought Larry, while reviewing all of his notes late on a Sunday evening. When he compared his notes to the outline that Patricia had drawn on her chalkboard he realized that there were only three more areas to discuss: conflict resolution, team members believing they are winners and being seen as a winning team by others. He resolved to contact Patricia immediately to learn about these three areas.

Step 8

PROBLEM SOLVING/CONFLICT RESOLUTION

A few weeks later Larry met with Patricia to review his notes on the Ten Minute Team and to ask about the additional characteristics of a high performing team. After exchanging greetings and agreeing on their agenda, Patricia asked, "Do you have any further observations or questions about the last team meeting?"

"I have been wondering specifically if having team members give other members advice on how to run their teams can lead to conflict and generally, how you handle conflict on the Ten Minute Team. I know that conflict is part of a team's process and I believe that to be high performing you have to handle conflict well."

"I agree with your observation," replied the Manager. "Conflict is a part of any team's process, and to be high performing you must handle conflict effectively. In response to your question, the answer is 'No'. There is very little risk of conflict when the team is assisting an individual to improve performance. All of the team members realize that the advice is intended to help and in most cases has been requested by the receiver.

"Handling conflict well is one mark of a high performing team," continued Patricia. "We are frequently handling conflicts, because in a high performing team there will be more disagreements and more alternatives proposed as solutions to a team problem. When team members feel free to speak their minds you have more opinions to deal with. This, however, provides for better decisions in almost all cases. Let me outline my beliefs about conflict management for you."

"Before you do that could you say more about what you mean by 'more disagreements, or more alternatives?' It sounds like you are equating problem solving and conflict resolution."

"You are correct," said the Manager. "Conflict management and problem solving are parts of the same process. If you have a problem to solve, there will always be at least two possible solutions, or you do not have a problem. Even when there is only one solution, there are always various ways to implement that solution. When you are choosing between alternatives you have a potential conflict situation, even though in some cases the conflict will not emerge. I believe, however, that to get the best solution there needs to be a debate between alternatives as a way to test the popular choice. When the debate fails to occur, the solution will always be weaker than it could have been.

"In a high performing team where all the team members feel free to state their opinion, you can expect that there will be differing opinions regarding any problem. That is one of the reasons high performing teams are high performing. They consider alternatives, debate them and select the best alternative, which has been strengthened by the debate. In addition, the team has been strengthened by the debate."

"I think I understand what you are saying, but I still don't know how a conflict can strengthen a team. Won't conflict destroy a team?" asked Larry.

"Conflict can destroy a team which hasn't spent time learning how to deal with it," replied Patricia. "There are several steps, however, which will help any team to handle conflicts better. Let me list them for you on the board."

The Manager listed the following steps:

1. *Satisfy minimum high performing team requirements*

   a. *develop trust*

   b. *develop minimum communication skills*

   c. *have a method for solving problems*

2. *Have a structured way to handle conflicts*

   a. *let each person state his/her view briefly—no filibustering*

   b. *have neutral team members identify areas of agreement and disagreement*

   c. *explore areas of disagreement for specific issues*

   d. *have opponents suggest modifications to their own and to the other's point of view*

   e. *if blocked ask opponents if they can accept the team's decision*

3. *Formally summarize and record the decision*

While she was writing, Larry copied the material into his notes. When the Manager finished, he commented, "That's a very simple process. I am going to try it this afternoon with my team. Can you tell me how you link this to problem solving?"

"I have a better idea," replied the Manager. "I'm meeting later this week with Jan, Cecelia, Bill and Chris to discuss an engineering change in Bill's area. I expect there will be a wide diversity of ideas. And as you may recall from attending the staff meeting, Bill and Chris have had disagreements before."

"I would like to be there," replied Larry, "I have to check my work before saying yes."

The meeting occurred a few afternoons later in Chris' office so the group could review his engineers' sketches of the production line changes. Bill arrived a few minutes late. His only comment was to remark, "It is a long way from where the real work is done to the ivory tower where the engineers live."

Larry noticed that Chris frowned but did not respond. When greetings had been exchanged the Manager suggested that since this was an engineering meeting that Chris should chair it. He agreed and began by reviewing the rationale for the changes, the process that his engineers were using and their progress to date. He concluded by saying, "If there are no questions maybe the group should look at some overheads which show the current production line and the proposed changes."

Without waiting for anyone else to comment Bill said, "Before we go ahead, someone better ask the supervisor on that line if any changes are needed." A silence followed.

Then Chris responded, "I was afraid this would happen. You have refused to meet with my engineers, you haven't commented on any of the proposed changes which I sent you and now you object to proceeding."

Bill quickly and angrily responded, "That is not true. Your engineers never talked to me. Besides they were usually there in the afternoon when I was away. I would have commented on the proposals if they had arrived before yesterday. You staff people think all we have to do is comment on your proposals!"

"It sounds like you two still haven't learned how to cooperate," said the Manager. "As I have told both of you, I will not accept your hassling each other. In the long run it's going to cost the entire team. For this meeting to be productive we should set aside the agenda of reviewing the proposed changes and hear from Bill and Chris about the need for the changes. Then we can review the proposals, if indeed change is appropriate. Now, Bill what is your view about the need for change?"

"Before I get into that, I guess I should apologize for my attitude. But it seems like where my area is concerned I just don't get consulted about changes," he replied.

"Do you want to apologize?" asked the Manager, following up on his first comment.

"Yes for my attitude. I'm sorry Chris, I know you are doing the best you can. But I am not apologizing for what I said. I'm not sure the changes are necessary and I don't feel like I have been involved in the process," Bill said.

Chris frowned, looked at his papers, and then addressed the Manager, "You are correct, Bill and I need to stop hassling each other, and maybe I should involve him some more."

"Why don't you tell Bill directly," Patricia suggested.

"Bill, I think we need to stop hassling each other and I will work harder to see that you are involved when I do projects which affect you," Chris said, while looking directly at Bill.

The Manager looked first at Bill then at Chris and said, "I'm pleased with what has just happened. You are both valuable members of our team and for the team to perform well each of you has a part to play. More importantly, you have a joint part where you work together. I think today will help in that regard. Now let's turn to the question of the need for changes. We will use our regular process for managing conflicting opinions. Bill, you begin."

"I'll begin by saying that we believe with a little more maintenance of the line, and with closer monitoring by the operators we can meet the production specifications without any modifications. Besides, another problem is that the modifications are going to take the line down for several hours a day for the next several weeks. We can't afford to have the line down and the unit idle," Bill stated.

"My position, as you might expect is quite different," said Chris. "We believe that the line will only have to be down for one to two hours for six days to make the modifications. We believe that more maintenance and better monitoring might allow the line to run at the manufacturer's specifications. However, with the modifications we can exceed those specs and require less maintenance. Finally, the operators told my engineers that they couldn't monitor the area where the problem exists because of a protective housing and safety shield. So, we think that for a small shutdown we can obtain longer term gains."

The Manager turned to Cecelia and Jan, who had been silent up to this point and asked if they could identify any areas of agreement or disagreement between Bill and Chris.

Cecelia said, "There are two areas of disagreement: the length of the shutdown and the benefits to be gained by the modifications."

"I see an important area of agreement," said Jan. "They both indicated that something more needs to be done to keep the line running. They disagree on the best approach."

"I agree with your observations," said the Manager. "Now maybe Bill and Chris can offer modifications to their own stances and to each other's. Why don't you continue Bill."

"I would be willing to withdraw my idea about more maintenance and better monitoring, based on what Chris reported from my operators. And, I would like to modify his idea about the amount of time it will take, because that is my real concern. I think it will take more than five days. Ten half days is more realistic, and I will resist a ten day shutdown, even for two hours a day," stated Bill.

"I'm delighted that we both agree that some change is needed," said Chris. "I expect that Bill is right about the amount of time the modifications will take. I am usually overly optimistic. I don't know if this would be possible, but if your real concern is shutting the line down maybe we could do the modifications at night, even though it would mean overtime and probably some extraordinary costs for night work. How does that sound?"

Jan responded instantly, "I had been thinking about the cost of the lost productivity for the two weeks that the modifications would probably require. Even if we could recover some of the pro- duction on each shift, I believe the loss would more than offset any overtime costs caused by doing the modifications at night."

"That would certainly take care of my problems," said Bill. "And if the modifications occur at night then

I have several other minor modifications I would like to discuss with the engineers. I like the idea and would like to meet with Chris when we are finished reviewing his proposals, to plan the schedule."

"I agree," said Chris.

"To complete the process, would you quickly write down your perceptions of the agreements for Bill to review," the Manager asked Chris.

Chris spent a minute making notes which he handed to Bill. After reading them Bill nodded his agreement, and handed the paper to the Manager, who clipped it to her pad.

"Here is the first slide showing the proposed modification," said Chris, as he began his presentation.

*   *   *   *   *

At the end of the meeting as Patricia and Larry were walking back to her office Larry said, "I certainly learned a lot about the value of having a process for handling conflicts. I also saw how valuable your role was in setting expectations for cooperation and in insuring that Bill and Chris stuck to the process. I also noticed that you didn't influence the discussion in any direction or offer your observations about the conflict."

"That's correct," Patricia responded. "I see the leader's job on a high performing team as providing expectations, providing helpful structures and facilitating members' participation. In a conflict, if I added my opinion it would be too likely to shift the decision in one direction. The result would be that one team member might feel like he lost and in addition, that the boss was against him. At the same time other team members would miss their opportunity to contribute.

No, on a high performing team, the leader's job isn't to make the decisions. However, part of the job is to see that others make good decisions."

"I'm surprised how quickly Bill and Chris reached an agreement today," said Larry, redirecting the conversation. It only took a few minutes for them to clarify the problem and to agree on some steps. I think it was less than ten minutes. That would never happen in my plant, so I wonder if it was a real problem. It was just too easy!"

"Yes, it did look easy," responded Patricia. "However, both Bill and Chris have experience resolving conflicts. In addition, if you ask them if it was easy I am sure they will say 'No', that it was a difficult few minutes but that the meeting was more productive as a result of the conflict."

"Are there some other techniques you use for problem solving which weren't used today?" asked Larry after a long pause to consider the Manager's response.

"There are," replied the Manager. "However, the most important step in problem solving is to be sure you are solving the correct problem. For example, in today's meeting we could have easily gotten into a debate about the need for changes, when the real problem was making the changes in a way which required the least downtime on the line.

"Our Ten Minute Team exercise is to first have each team member state the problem as they see it. We then take a minute or two to get an agreement on a working statement. Usually there will be a consensus, even though one or two team members may have a slightly different perspective.

"We then go around again and allow up to one minute for each team member to make a solution statement. Again there is often a pretty clear solution favored by most of the team. At this point I would probably assign the problem to the team members most involved for further work."

"What happens if the problem is one where all of the team members need to be involved?" asked Larry.

"In those cases we agree on the steps of the problem solving process we are going to use as a team. For example, we may decide to do problem identification, solution generation, selection of likely alternatives and pros and cons of each alternative as a group. In this case we would allocate no more than ten minutes to each step in the process. Generally, we would begin each step by going around the team to get ideas from each member. Then when we had heard from everyone we would have some open discussion, but would continually seek a consensus to enable us to move to the next step in the process," explained the Manager.

"Remember, in each step in the problem solving process we are also resolving conflicts."

"That sounds a lot more efficient than the discussions my team gets into," said Larry. "Don't you miss some important information being so efficient?"

"We actually miss less information than most teams," responded Patricia. "The reasons are that we are seeking a solution rather than posturing or lobbying for personal viewpoints and we hear from everyone. So we spend less time on debates which are ego driven. By listening to each other there is no need for a person to continually make the same point.

"And, anytime someone has a new idea they are free to bring it up. We are different from many teams in this respect, where once the discussion has moved on it isn't appropriate to bring up a new point. We recognize that some team members are more thoughtful than others and that they may take longer to sort through the information. Knowing this we will not move ahead until we have heard from everyone. However, even then it is all right to add new ideas later."

"I certainly like that!" exclaimed Larry. "Sometimes I feel like my meetings are just a debate between two or three loudmouths, and if I don't get my ideas in quickly then it is too late. I often just turn off. Are there any other problem solving techniques you use?"

"I have team members give ten minute reports on new problem solving techniques, and sometimes we will take ten minutes to do a puzzle or play a game which requires team problem solving, then we will compare how we behaved in the game with our normal approach to problem solving," replied the Manager. "Sometimes we learn a lot from the game, but at the very least we have a few minutes of fun as a team."

"This has been a very useful discussion," said Larry. "I've learned a lot about problem solving this afternoon."

That evening as Larry reviewed his notes he noted the following points related to problem solving.

- *Be sure you are solving the right problem.*

- *Have a specific problem solving process, do not rely on discussion alone.*

- *Be task focused and directed, but allow new ideas to be introduced.*

- *Get everyone's opinion and insure that everyone listens.*

- *Learn new problem solving methods.*

- *Use puzzles and games to develop problem solving skills.*

"It certainly helps to think about conflict as a natural part of solving problems," Larry thought as he closed his folder.

Step 9

BELIEVING WE ARE WINNERS
(TEAM SPIRIT)

A call to Patricia on Monday resulted in a meeting for Wednesday to discuss winning. At work on Monday Larry discovered that his team had missed a production deadline. After a meeting with his boss and a meeting with his team members he felt discouraged and anxious about his own ability and that of his team. He wondered if his team was a loser rather than a winner.

Larry began the meeting with Patricia by relating his concerns about his own team and his confusion about winning and losing. Patricia listened until he was finished and then leaned forward and said, "I think this is a marvelous time for you to learn about turning an apparent loss into a win."

"I would like that, but am not sure how to go about it," Larry responded quietly.

"First of all you only missed the deadline by a few hours, and you were able to provide the necessary numbers and quality," said the Manager. "To begin feeling like winners you need to focus on everything your team did which was correct. I think you will discover that most of their efforts were focused in the right direction and contributed to completing the production task. During the process of reviewing what you did right you will discover where additional effort, or effort slightly redirected would have enabled you to meet the deadline. More importantly, however, focusing on what you have done which was correct helps all of you to begin to feel like winners and not losers."

"I've been taught to dig into problems, find out what went wrong and make changes so the problems won't occur again," protested Larry.

"We have all been taught that process," responded Patricia. "However, problem focusing almost always leads to a narrow focus which in turn often leads to fixing the wrong thing or to missing a larger system flaw. A much better approach is to focus on the goal and see where you need to improve to accomplish it. Even when you fix the right problem the impact on a team of focusing on problems is devastating. It almost always results in looking for a person on which to place blame, in a feeling of depression, and in having the team focus in the future on preventing problems rather than on winning."

"I certainly agree with that," responded Larry. "My manager even asked me to prepare a paper with recommendations for how not to miss deadlines. I would like to see us focused on winning, rather than just getting by."

"One of the real characteristics of high performing teams is their focus on very high goals," responded Patricia. "They are intent on scoring on each play rather than just gaining yardage or getting to first base. We are often taught to set goals which are high but attainable. The result of this advice is that goals are usually set which are attainable, but not very challenging. In addition, most teams have never had an experience of being high performing so they set goals which match their limited vision of their potential.

"I have my team set goals which will translate into a real win, not a small gain. Then we monitor our progress against those goals constantly and ask how we can work smarter to get the win."

"What you are saying sounds good, but I'm not sure how to begin," said Larry after a pause.

"You begin by having your team thoroughly discuss what they have done which was successful and what they did to be successful. There is a popular adage about learning from your mistakes. Well, I think about all you learn from your mistakes is how not to make that particular mistake again. You don't learn much about how to be successful. So I stress learning from our successes," stated Patricia forcefully.

"Last year I was on a task force to review our project management system," Larry said excitedly, "and we decided to review the most successful projects and to build a list of the factors which had contributed to the success of those projects. It was a very positive experience for all of us. And what's more, when we were finished we had a model for running a successful project and at the same time we had discovered why some of the less successful projects had failed.

"One particular project manager had been criticized for not being forceful enough with outside suppliers since his project was always slipping behind waiting for materials. Well, we discovered that the Company's project scheduling cycle was too short and rather than having a problem with one manager we really had a problem which could affect all projects. So far we had been lucky."

"Larry, what can you learn about helping your team to feel like they are winners from that experience?" asked the Manager.

"First, looking at factors leading to success was very exciting for all of us," Larry responded. "Second, by looking at success factors we discovered the reasons for previous problems. It was a building process and not one of looking for someone or something to blame.

"This discussion is helpful in thinking about a way to manage," said Larry. "Are there other things you do to help your team feel like a winner?"

"There are several things we do regularly," responded Patricia with a smile. "Some of them may seem silly, so let me provide a perspective first.

"We talked earlier about team spirit and how sports teams develop that spirit. There are some very common techniques that sports teams at all levels use to tell their players they are winners. Some examples are pep rallies, cheerleaders, cheers, chants, awards in the form of letters, rings, and contracts, player of the week, most valuable player, posting of newspaper articles and all the interpersonal support among team members, pats on the back, high fives, etc."

"But, wait..." interrupted Larry.

"I know what you're thinking," said the Manager. "That stuff is OK for sports, but this is business. True, but business tends to borrow many of its team models from sports, so why exclude some of the ingredients which make athletic teams successful," asked the Manager rhetorically.

"Well, I don't know," said Larry. "I could see giving awards, but cheerleaders! That just wouldn't work."

"That's one of your jobs as a supervisor," said Patricia. "As well as coaching, you also need to cheerlead. If you have the time I would like to have you talk to my team members and let them tell you about some of the other ways we help each other to feel like winners. You can call them to see when they are available."

"I'd like to do that, but I'm a little skeptical," he replied.

Larry was able to schedule a meeting with Dorothy, one of the production supervisors, for the next day. When he arrived she said that she had invited Marcus, from Packaging, to join them. After a few minutes of small talk about Larry's plant and common supervision problems, Larry said that he had asked for the meeting to discuss what the TMT did to promote feeling like winners.

"That's easy," said Marcus. "We support each other every way we can. Team members are always offering to help with both personal and work problems. I feel like a winner because they let me know their support is there for me."

"That is true for me as well," said Dorothy thoughtfully. "As you both know there were times in the past few months when I didn't feel like a winner because of my unit's productivity. The thing which made a difference for me was that all of the team, and especially the Manager let me know that they thought I could be a winner. So, for me the support was very important.

"However, I also remember, very clearly, the team meeting where Patricia asked each of us to list all the accomplishments and successes we had from the previous month. I surprised myself at how long my list was. I guess I had been focused on my problems and had not had time to review my successes. I started feeling more like a winner during that meeting."

"That sounds like bragging and I don't feel comfortable doing that," said Larry. "I usually shrug or laugh off my successes."

"That's just the problem," Dorothy said quickly. "We focus on the weaknesses and problems but laugh off the successes. No wonder so many people feel like losers and not winners. Besides, it is true that you need to blow your own horn."

"Well, I can see how acknowledging individual and team success can help the team and team members feel like winners. I would like to see more of that in my team," said Larry. "But Patricia talked about cheerleading and pep rallies. I can't see how that fits into business."

"That's exactly how I felt when I joined the TMT," responded Marcus. "But when we start talking about our successes and some of our goals, I get really excited. It does remind me of my college track team. We were really good and sometimes after we talked about how good we were and what we could accomplish if we really tried, we actually performed better.

"When a team member tells me they think I can accomplish something and that they are with me, it feels a little like having cheerleaders. In fact, last month when I had to make a presentation to management and Bill and Jan asked to attend with me, I felt more confident because my cheerleaders were there to support me."

"When you say it that way it doesn't sound silly," said Larry. "What else do you do to feel like winners?"

"Last week we had an awards ceremony," said Dorothy. "I received a red ribbon for my courage in setting higher production goals than my unit had ever achieved. I think it's neat to get recognition for the little things. Now, I'm even more committed to seeing that we achieve those goals."

"Were there other awards?" asked Larry.

"Yes, everyone received an award for something," answered Dorothy. "Chris received $100 from the Manager for the cost savings which resulted from his engineering changes in Bill's area. He then offered to buy pizza for Bill and his unit as a sign of his appreciation for their cooperation."

"Aren't you a little disappointed getting a ribbon when Chris received a $100?" asked Larry.

"Not really. What is important is that each of us received an award which had personal meaning to us. In this way we are all winners. Sometimes the award is humorous but it always relates to the individual and lets him/her know that s/he has made an important contribution to the team. Besides, the last time we had awards I received a free weekend in the mountains. So over time all of us receive significant awards."

"What else do you do to feel like winners?" Larry asked, looking up from his notes.

"Well it's a little like the awards ceremony. Any team member can give another team member a gold star if you think that team member has done something which warrants recognition. I'm often surprised when I get one. I think that I'm just doing my job, then someone else gives me a star and I realize I have been doing a better job than I thought. Then I attempt to do better. It is a cycle. If you recognize someone for their work, they work harder and then they get more recognition. Pretty soon we all feel more like winners," said Marcus.

"We also discuss other people's statements about winning and achieving," said Dorothy. "Last week we spent a few minutes discussing a comment our company president made. He said 'Winning isn't everything but it beats the alternatives.' We decided that sometimes it may be more important to feel like winners than to actually win. You can't always win but it is important that the team members continue to feel like they are winners. Sometimes one of us will bring a quote from a famous person about winning and discuss it. These discussions help us to clarify our team's philosophy and our strategy for achieving our goals."

"This has been helpful," said Larry. "I think I understand a lot more about the importance of a team feeling like a winner, and how to use some simple techniques to develop that feeling. Thanks for your time."

Later that day as Larry was working on his notes he listed the following points:

- *Focusing on winning leads to a better solution than focusing on problem prevention.*

- *Focusing on winning lifts a team's morale.*

- *Set high goals and regularly assess progress toward those goals.*

- *By using simple techniques team members will feel like winners.*

  - *Give awards to all team members for accomplishments.*

  - *Have team members provide gold stars to each other.*

  - *Discuss other people's statements about winning.*

  - *Affirm team and members with positive support.*

"I think I now understand some of the enthusiasm and energy in the TMT," he thought. "They see themselves as winners. They have team spirit."

Step 10

BEING SEEN AS WINNERS
(IMAGE)

Early the following week Larry scheduled a meeting with Patricia to talk about how a team gets to be seen by others as a winning team.

As usual Patricia was available when Larry arrived. After they had exchanged greetings he commented about her punctuality. Her response startled him.

"How do you think punctuality relates to your question about being seen as a winner?" she asked

"Well, I'm eh, not really sure," he answered hesitantly. "Is being on time the same as being a winner?" he asked.

"Not really," she answered with a smile. "But, always doing what you say you are going to do and keeping your commitments to others is part of being seen as a winner. I have found that when I commit to a deadline, a meeting, or a production quota I am promising someone else that I will perform in a certain manner. When I do perform they begin to see that I am a person whom they can trust not to disappoint them. Over time they begin to not only trust me but to count on me to do as I say. Thus, I become a reliable part of their environment. And as such their lives are made easier. So, in a way punctuality symbolizes being a winner."

"I've never thought about winning like that," responded Larry thoughtfully. "I certainly begin to see people as losers when they fail to deliver on their promises. After awhile I just write them off.

"What else do you do to get the TMT seen as a winning team?" asked Larry.

"I anticipate questions," said Patricia with a grin. "So today I have another meeting scheduled for you with Mr. Garcia. You can talk to him about how he sees us and what he thinks we do to be seen as winners. Come back after your meeting and we can talk further."

                    *   *   *   *   *

"Well, my favorite supervisor! I wondered if you were still around. How's Pat and the TMT? Sit down and ask your questions," said Mr. Garcia in his hearty voice.

"I guess we're all fine," said Larry attempting to answer Mr. Garcia's questions. "I want to talk to you again about the TMT. Actually, I want to know how you see them and what you think their image is in the company."

"I thought we talked about that last time. I told you I think they are a top notch team. What else do you need to know?" asked Mr. Garcia.

"Well, I have been talking to Patricia about the team's image in the rest of the company and how the team's behavior contributes to shaping the image," said Larry feeling pleased that he was able to respond to Mr. Garcia without being nervous.

"They have a winning image in the company. And they deserve it because they deliver. If they promise me a batch of product by a certain date they deliver it," said Mr. Garcia emphatically. "They will negotiate with me about realistic time frames and production quotas, but once we reach an agreement they always perform as well or better than I expect.

"I don't know if this is related to what you are asking about, but I have the belief about the TMT that I always get what I want. They may push back and bargain, but when we reach an agreement I don't worry about them delivering."

"What else do you see them doing which contributes to their image of being a winning team?" asked Larry.

"Well, they are certainly positive. Even when I make demands on them, which I think are unreasonable, they respond with a *can do* attitude. They must think they can do anything.

"They are very positive about each other. They let me know when one of the team members has been successful. For example, I'll bet you didn't know that Chris made some engineering changes which may save the company over $100,000 this year. Or that Jan was just elected vice-president of the local accounting society.

"I don't think I've ever heard them complain. And they certainly never complain about each other. One time last year they were having problems with one of their units and I knew it," stated Mr. Garcia. "I needed a rush delivery and I expected they would tell me they couldn't deliver because of the unit. Instead, Cecelia negotiated a staggered delivery schedule and I never heard a word about their problems. I liked that. My view of Cecelia's abilities certainly went up a notch."

"Is there anything else?" asked Larry.

"It's a little thing, but they all look very respectable," responded Mr. Garcia thoughtfully. "If you know what I mean."

"I'm not sure I do," said Larry.

"Well, sometimes people dress poorly, or need a haircut, or just have bad taste. Don't get me wrong, I wouldn't hold that against a person," said Mr. Garcia quickly. "But with the TMT you never see any of those things. How they look makes a difference in how they are seen.

"Well is there anything else you needed to know?" Mr.Garcia asked without a pause.

"I don't think so. Thanks for your time," Larry responded.

"Any time. As I said last time, I love to talk to rookie supervisors," said Mr. Garcia with a grin.

When Larry was seated in Patricia's office she asked with a smile, "What did he say, I can hardly wait."

"He said that you and the TMT:

- *Deliver what you promise.*
- *Make others feel like they are right in what they want.*
- *Act positive and have a can do attitude.*
- *Never talk negatively about the TMT or team members.*
- *Look respectable.*

"Those points all sound like things we attempt to do," said Patricia. "Do you have questions about any of them?"

"Not specific ones, but I am interested in your comments," said Larry.

"Mr. Garcia's observation about delivering is correct. Delivering what we promise is the critical activity if a team is to be seen as a winner. It has to perform. I know it sounds obvious, but unless a team produces what it promises, it cannot be a winning team," Patricia responded.

"I also agree with his comment about him feeling like he gets what he wants. The TMT believes that the customer is always right. That doesn't mean that we attempt to respond to everyone's requests; we will negotiate and work to make demands realistic, but in the final analysis we attempt to meet the customer's needs.

"But, you know, it isn't enough to just do a good job," she said reflectively. "There are always teams and individuals who do a good job, who don't get the recognition and rewards. In addition to doing a good job you have to shape your public image. So when Mr. Garcia said that we tell him about our successes he was accurate. We do it intentionally. We want the rest of the organization to know that we are good."

"Isn't that kind of egotistical; bragging about doing your job?" asked Larry with a frown. "I know people who are always talking big but rarely deliver."

"It may seem egotistical, but it is no different from any successful organization making its story public. We want to build our reputation through good work, but in a busy organization good work often gets overlooked. We don't want to be overlooked when projects are assigned and promotions considered. So, we believe it is important to share our successes with others in the organization," Patricia said.

"I can see your point," Larry said. "I know a team in my plant that does a super job. While everyone sees

them as productive they are not seen as high performing even though their production records are some of
the best in the division. Is there anything else you do
to maintain your image?"

"As Mr. Garcia mentioned, we pay attention to our
total image. We give each other feedback on dress and
style. We never talk negatively about a team member
to people outside the team. Also, we never intentionally
discredit any other member of the organization. This
way we work both to promote a positive image and to
avoid a negative image.

"Even though it is difficult at times, we always
attempt to be optimistic. I want team members to project an image that we are willing to tackle problems
and that we believe we can solve them. Then a member
can come to the rest of the team and we will work to
produce what has been promised."

"I'm always surprised how our morale is improved
when we take a positive attitude," said Patricia. "When
we appear positive to the rest of the organization, we
seem to be more optimistic as a team. We believe the
glass is half full, not half empty."

"I know how I hate working with people who are
always pessimistic and gloomy," interjected Larry.

"Sometimes we give ourselves a treat which bolsters
our image as winners. Often this helps to project the
image to the rest of the organization. I remember once
last year when we had been working with lots of tough
issues and energy was low. Bill suggested that we
dress up for a week. His statement was, 'Just because
we had all been in the trenches there was no excuse
for looking that way.' Well, by dressing a little better,
we all felt better and several of our colleagues in the

organization commented that we must have just set some new records. They didn't know why we were dressed up but assumed that we had had another success. The same principle applies to reports, presentation material and work areas. If your area is a mess people will begin to see you as a mess."

"I think you are saying that being seen as a winner is a combination of high performance and managed image," Larry summarized.

"That is an oversimplified summary," Patricia responded, "Are there any specific points you noted?"

Larry looked at his notes for a minute and then said, "In addition to the points I mentioned at the beginning of the meeting I have added the following ideas from you."

- *A team needs to market its accomplishments.*
- *Consult with other team members about style and dress, materials, work area, etc.*
- *Do some special activities to show that you are winners, like the week you dressed up.*

"I like that summary better," said Patricia with a smile.

After a slight pause, Larry closed his note pad and looked directly at Patricia. "I really don't know how to thank you and the Ten Minute Team for all of your time and help. I've learned more than I ever expected, and I know I'm already a better supervisor. I would like to meet occasionally to let you know how my team is progressing."

"I would enjoy that, Larry. I have certainly gotten clearer about high performing teams since you joined us. Having you ask questions and share observations has sharpened my understanding of building a high performing team. I know that I could train someone else to become a Ten Minute Team Leader faster and more accurately then I could have before. Good Luck!"

PERFORMANCE INDICATORS

Several months passed while Larry worked with his team on the Ten Minute Team process and worked with them to raise their level of performance. As near as he could tell all of the TMT factors were in place, but he wasn't sure that his team had actually become high performing. Maybe Patricia had some ideas for measuring team performance. He decided to set up a meeting.

Patricia sounded pleased to hear from Larry and agreed to an early morning meeting the following week.

After catching up on the highlights of their past few months Larry asked the question that had been bothering him.

"How do you know if your team is high performing? What are the indicators?" Without waiting for an answer he went on, "I think my team is working very well. We know who our key customers are, we review the list regularly, the trust level seems high and we have very few conflicts. So I think we are high performing, but I'm just not sure. How will I know?"

Patricia chuckled, "Your question is one indicator of your progress. A few months ago you were attempting to define a high performing team and today you are concerned about performance measures. I would say that is progress."

"Well yes, but I need some specific ways of telling if we are high performing."

"There are some indicators I use that tell me how my team is doing," Patricia replied. "I have four direct indicators and I have developed several ratios to measure progress. Let me list them on the board." Patricia made the following list.

Direct Indicators:

1.   Are we attending to the TMT factors?
2.   Are we meeting our team or functional goals?
3.   Are team members being considered for promotion or transfer?
4.   Are we quick at reaching decisions, responding to customers and completing projects?

Ratios:

1.   Ratio of team to individual turf conversations.
2.   Ratio of team members who readily volunteer for extra tasks to those who hold back.
3.   Ratio of future-focused to past-focused items on the team meeting agenda.
4.   Ratio of anticipated events to surprises.
5.   Ratio of issues taken care of by team members in pairs and subgroups to those brought to the full team.

"I understand the first four even though I had never thought about team members being considered for promotion as an indicator of team performance. I think I understand the ratios but would like to talk about them," Larry said after reading the list. "I don't see how you can measure everything required to compute the ratios."

"It isn't always possible to directly obtain the numbers for the ratios so I have to rely on my observations, what I hear indirectly from team members and what I know from direct experience. For example, I don't always know when team members have solved problems between themselves without bringing them to the team. On the other hand, I can count the agenda items to determine the ratio of future to past items. I am looking for positive numbers, so I divide the first item in each pair by the second. As we get better the ratio gets bigger, and if we slip the ratio gets smaller," Patricia said. She paused and waited for Larry's next question.

"I would like to talk a little about each item if you have the time. By team versus individual turf do you mean the number of times that team members place the team's interest ahead of their own area?"

"That is exactly what I mean," responded Patricia. "There are times when it is important for a team member to advocate his or her own area, but in general that leads to divisiveness and lowers team performance. Often I see members begin by discussing the needs of their area and then when everyone has spoken they make decisions on what is best for the team. As the team leader it is easy for me to recognize what the members are doing. If I see too much focus on individual turf I bring it to the team's attention."

"What about volunteering versus holding back? I have heard that it isn't always a good idea to be volunteering."

"Larry, I'm surprised at that statement. There are always tasks which need to be done that do not fall in any single team member's area. On most teams there are one or two members who will always take on extra work. On a high performing team all the members readily take on extra work even though they may complain about how busy they are. When more members on a team begin to volunteer, the work gets distributed more evenly and the entire team benefits. When I am in other meetings and no one volunteers for the extra task, I know that I am in a low performing team. Again, as the team leader it is easy to note the ratio of volunteering to holding back."

"That is a great ratio!" exclaimed Larry after a pause. "And I have seen my team change in a positive direction. When I first became supervisor I would ask for help with a new task and everyone would sit until I asked someone to take the assignment. I have seen a shift during the past two months where nearly everyone is taking on extra work. I think that as we get better as a team, team members may have more time and certainly more commitment to the team. Maybe that encourages them to volunteer.

"I have also seen some evidence of your last ratio, taking care of problems in pairs and trios rather than bringing everything to the team. I hadn't thought of that as a measure of increased team performance, but as I think about it I suppose working issues in sub-teams indicates a higher level of trust between the members, and maybe even more trust in me. They know that I won't be upset. They would also have to have more communication skills and be familiar with a problem solving method. You were right about not always knowing. I don't know everything that gets handled outside the full team, but I know that fewer issues seem to be on our agenda these days."

Patricia smiled as Larry continued to think out loud about his team's progress. When he paused she said, "In that case I expect that you are also improving the other two ratios—fewer surprises and more future-focused items on the agenda."

"We haven't had any surprises lately. I think that is because we are getting really good at working with our key customers in the organization. I know we avoided a major problem last month because we had been talking to the materials people and knew they were anticipating a shortage of a vital chemical. We were able to plan for the shortage without losing any production. That was really different than when I started. We seemed to be getting hit by surprises and changes every week. So I think we are becoming more high performing based on that ratio."

"What about future-focused versus past-focused items?" asked Patricia.

"I don't think we do very well in that area. In fact there are some items which have been on our agenda for a few meetings which are planning items. We seem to always be focused on current ones and a few past ones. The future items don't have enough pressure."

"That's often the case. In a first level team it isn't unusual to have lots of current issues, since you are working directly with the product. At my level I need to have more future items and fewer current items. However, neither of us should have many items which focus on the past, unless we are doing a review in order to plan. It sounds like we have uncovered an area where you might want to focus more as the team leader," said Patricia.

"We have uncovered more than that," Larry said with a grin. "I have discovered, with your help, ways to confirm what I suspected—my team is getting better! Now I have some means of measuring how well we are doing. Let me review them before I leave."

Larry had the following measures listed in his notebook:

A high performing team...
- *attends to the TMT elements.*
- *achieves its team or functional goals.*
- *has team members who are being considered for promotion or transfer.*
- *is quick at reaching decisions, responding to customers and completing projects.*

Ratios

- <u>*team needs*</u>
  individual turf

- <u>*team members who volunteer*</u>
  team members who hold back

- <u>*future-focused agenda items*</u>
  past-focused agenda items

- <u>*anticipated events*</u>
  surprises

- <u>*issues taken care of by sub-teams*</u>
  issues brought to the full team

"I wonder if I could get my manager to accept this as part of my performance review," Larry said jokingly as he closed his folder. "Once again, I really appreciate your time and interest."

"Your questions help me continue to learn. Call any-time," said Patricia extending her hand.

BUILDING A HIGH PERFORMING TEAM:
A SUMMARY AND OVERHEADS

A few weeks later Larry received a message to call the Plant Manager. His first reaction was to review what he might have done wrong. His second was to realize that the first reaction was probably groundless. Nevertheless his call was placed with some anxiety. He was relieved at the Plant Manager's greeting.

"Larry, I have been hearing great things about you and your team and wonder if you could help me out. The main agenda for the next company-wide Plant Manager's meeting is team development. I want you to come along and do a presentation about the way you have developed your team. By the way, this is all cleared with your manager."

Larry's anxiety changed to relief and pleasure at the compliment and then back to anxiety as he thought about presenting to the Plant Managers. "Of course I will help. I'm very pleased at being asked. May I come to your office to get the details and in particular to clarify your expectations?"

Later that afternoon Larry began to prepare for the presentation by reviewing all of the notes he had made while meeting with Patricia and the TMT. His summaries seemed to form an outline.

As Larry reviewed his notes he began to draft overheads to provide him with material for the presentation at the Plant Managers meeting. He also knew that learning to develop a high performing team was going to help his career more than he had ever imagined. This presentation is just the first step.

*   *   *   *   *

LARRY'S SUMMARY OVERHEADS FOR BUILDING A HIGH PERFORMING TEAM

(You may use them for your team)

Model for a High Performing Team.

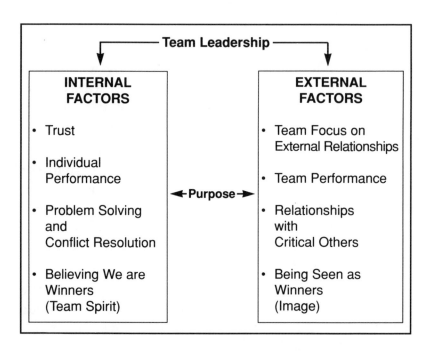

OVERVIEW OF A HIGH PERFORMING TEAM

- High performing teams need both an *internal* and *external* focus.

- There are *four elements* which contribute to *internal excellence:* trust, individual performance, problem solving/conflict resolution, and team members believing we are a winner.

- There are *four elements* which contribute to *external excellence:* identifying critical others, team performance, relationships with critical others, and being seen as winners.

- The leader's task is to help the team keep all of the elements in focus.

- Focus is maintained by regularly reviewing each element in a Ten Minute Team session.

- Finally, if the team has problems with an element in a review session, that is an indication that more attention needs to be paid to that element.

THE TMT PROCESS

- Each team member knows the Ten Minute Team task before the meeting.

- Each team member is prepared.

- Each team member makes her/his contribution.

- The leader makes her/his comments last.

- Discussion occurs after everyone has made individual contributions.

- Someone summarizes, the summary is amended and accepted.

ROLE OF THE LEADER OF A
HIGH PERFORMING TEAM

- The team leader must believe in teams.

- The team leader must state expectations about teamwork, and give praise and reprimands to support the expectations.

- The team leader must set aside time in team meetings to focus on the team's performance and development.

TEAM PURPOSE

- Teams must be clear on how they support organization purpose.

- Purpose provides daily guidance as well as future goals.

- Individuals should be able to see the link between their work, their team's purpose and the organization's purpose.

- Teams need to refocus on purpose from time to time.

IDENTIFYING CRITICAL OTHERS

- The team develops a list of critical others.
- The team regularly looks for additions, changes, deletions to the list.
- Recent events which may change the team's credibility are headlined.
- An individual is identified to work with each critical other.
- The team provides advice to that individual.
- If asked, the manager assists with strategy and action steps.

BUILDING RELATIONSHIPS WITH CRITICAL OTHERS

- You clarify the other person's performance expectations of your team.

- You get current feedback about your team's performance.

- You maintain a positive relationship with a critical person in the organization.

- You strengthen your team by having one of your subordinates be the primary link between you and the other person.

- Finally, you help the other manager improve his/her own team's performance, which helps everyone.

TRUST

- Trust is built by focusing directly on it.
- Taking risks is necessary to build trust.
- Getting supported for taking risks builds trust.
- Allowing yourself to be vulnerable increases others' trust of you.
- Caring about each other is necessary to establish trust.
- Letting go of negative incidents in the past is critical to trust building.

INDIVIDUAL PERFORMANCE

- It is unrealistic to expect to hire top performers for all of your jobs.

- The manager must reward teamwork and eliminate divisive behavior.

- Coaching and training are made available for each team member.

- Team members must see a problem of one member as a problem for the entire team, and therefore as their own problem.

- Someone publicly informs the entire team about a performance problem that needs attention.

- The team member with the performance problem discusses the concerns s/he has.

- Members offer resources, ideas and support which might help.

- Finally, the team member with the problem takes responsibility for utilizing the resources offered.

TEAM PERFORMANCE

- High performing teams anticipate important events.

- They rehearse, as a team, for the event.

- They play and learn together, i.e., a Ropes course or a supervisory skills course.

- Team members teach the rest of the team skills they acquire through training.

- Social activities as a team benefit the team.

- Job rotation and cross training help the team to perform at a higher level.

- High performing teams use nonrational methods to develop team spirit: breathing in unison, songs and pregame huddles.

PROBLEM SOLVING

- Be sure you are solving the right problem.

- Have a specific problem solving process, do not rely on discussion alone.

- Be task focused and directed, but allow new ideas to be introduced.

- Get everyone's opinion and insure that everyone listens.

- Learn new problem solving methods.

- Use puzzles and games to develop problem solving skills.

CONFLICT RESOLUTION

- Have a structured way to handle conflicts:
  - Let each person state his/her view briefly (no speechmaking).
  - Have neutral team members reflect areas of agreement and disagreement.
  - Explore areas of disagreement for specific issues.
  - Have opponents suggest modifications to own and others' points of view.
  - If blocked, ask opponents if they can accept the team's decision.
- Formally summarize and record the decision.

FEELING LIKE WINNERS

- Focusing on winning leads to a better solution than focusing on problem prevention.

- Focusing on winning lifts a team's morale.

- Set high goals and regularly assess progress toward those goals.

- By using simple techniques team members will feel like winners.

  - Give awards to all team members for accomplishments.

  - Have team members provide gold stars to each other.

  - Discuss other people's statements about winning.

  - Affirm team and members with positive support.

BEING SEEN BY OTHERS AS A WINNER

- Deliver what you promise.
- Make others feel like they are right in what they want.
- Act positive and have a *can do* attitude.
- Never talk negatively about the TMT or team members.
- Look respectable.
- Market the team's accomplishments.
- Consult with other team members about style and dress, materials, work area, etc.
- Do some special activities to show that you are winners (like the week the team dressed up).

PERFORMANCE MEASURES

A high performing team...

- *attends to the TMT elements.*
- *achieves its team or functional goals.*
- *has team members who are being considered for promotion or transfer.*
- *is quick at reaching decisions, responding to customers and completing projects.*

Ratios

- *team needs*
  individual turf

- *team members who volunteer*
  team members who hold back

- *future-focused agenda items*
  past-focused agenda items

- *anticipated events*
  surprises

- *issues taken care of by sub-teams*
  issues brought to the full team

About the Author

Thomas Isgar received his Ph.D. in Management from Purdue University with graduate work in Organizational Behavior at Case Western University. Dr. Isgar was on the Board of Directors of National Training Laboratories (NTL) and also on the Board of Certified Consultants International (CCI).

He has been an independent consultant for more than 20 years. National and international organizations he has assisted include Digital Equipment Company, DuPont, Penn Mutual, Boise Cascade, Exxon, Polaroid, the Telephone Company of Singapore and the Office of the Auditor General of Canada.

His areas of expertise include: management and team development, team leadership, performance appraisal, organizational design, conflict resolution, and socio-technical work redesign.

Tom is a member of a consulting firm owned by Susan Isgar. He has a son in college. In addition to work he enjoys tennis, running and skiing.